PSALMS FOR BIKERS

Vol. 1

Marty & Debbie Edwards

authorHOUSE®

AuthorHouse™
1663 Liberty Drive, Suite 200
Bloomington, IN 47403
www.authorhouse.com
Phone: 1-800-839-8640

First published by AuthorHouse 2/6/2008

ISBN: 978-1-4343-6925-3 (sc)

Library of Congress Control Number: 2008901198

Printed in the United States of America
Bloomington, Indiana

This book is printed on acid-free paper.

Dedicated

to

our two favorite people in the entire world.

Our sons,

Jonathan & Gabriel

CONTENTS

INTRODUCTION

It has been our privilege to ride motorcycles in some of the most beautiful places in America. We have chased the California coastline and navigated the Florida Keys. We have toured Maui and the infamous "road to Hana" and tempted the deserts of Nevada and Arizona to consume us. We have especially appreciated the canyons of Southern Utah (particularly Zion) with personal favorites including the back roads of Maine and New Hampshire. But what self-respecting biker would go without mentioning the Black Hills of South Dakota? Wherever we have ridden, we have embraced the ride, the view and the people.

Bikers are, in part, what makes riding so unforgettable. A few have given the majority a bad reputation while most are terrific people just out to celebrate the opportunity to be free in the wind. Though not particularly religious, we have found two wheelers to be curiously spiritual. Be it a bell dangling from their frame for good luck or the eagerness to have a bike "blessed" by a pastor or priest, bikers indeed have a spiritual dimension. We believe the explanation for this openness comes from a daily baptism of beauty and adventure. Unlike a car (or "cage" as some call it), two wheels expose ALL of our senses to nature. Who has ridden through the giant trees of Northern California and said with certainty, "There is no God!" Who has heard the thunder directly above them and not recognized a voice that was not their own? And which of us have not wondered how we escaped catastrophe by the grace of some unseen hand? There IS a God and he IS good and all that he has made is wonderful!

This book is a look at the first fifty Psalms of the Holy Bible and an attempt to apply its words to our lives out on the road. None of us is an island. No one can say that he has learned it all. The Psalms are a voice in the wilderness offering wisdom, truth, peace, protection and salvation. And even if you do not consider yourself a Christian, truth is still truth and there is much to be learned from those pages.

The book is small, ready to be tucked away in a coat or saddlebag. Each chapter is short, designed for a quick read on the side of the road. But the message will not stop when you close its covers. It will only begin a conversation in your mind between you and your maker. Read a little and then explore the back roads of your heart and mind as the Spirit of God rides alongside.

Marty & Debbie Edwards

PSALM 1

MAY I TINKER WITH YOUR BIKE?

1 Blessed is the man who does not walk in the counsel of the wicked or stand in the way of sinners or sit in the seat of mockers. 2 But his delight is in the law of the Lord, and on his law he meditates day and night. 3 He is like a tree planted by streams of water, which yields its fruit in season and whose leaf does not wither. Whatever he does prospers. 4 Not so the wicked! They are like chaff that the wind blows away. 5 Therefore the wicked will not stand in the judgment, nor sinners in the assembly of the righteous. 6 For the Lord watches over the way of the righteous, but the way of the wicked will perish.

We were all sitting at the local Harley dealership on a lazy Saturday afternoon chomping down free hotdogs and sodas, when Harry, with his mouth still full of his last bite, began to expound upon the mysteries of the universe. He can tell you everything there is to know about marriage because he's been married four times. And he's pretty good with the world of finance too because he's gone bankrupt…twice! He had not been yackin' long however, before Charlie chimed in with his version of all truth and wisdom. He assured us of its accuracy by reminding us that he heard it all from Ralph in the parts department.

Far fetched? Not really! How many of us have drawn our conclusions on life and eternity from something we heard someone say? Equally bad, we heard it on T.V. or the radio or read it in the newspaper. And how many times have you heard someone begin their "truth" with the words, "Well…it just seems to me..?" The Bible tells us however, **"There is a way that seems right to a man, but in the end it leads to death."** (Proverbs 14:12) Would you allow me to work on your bike based upon "what seems right to me?" or according to "what I've always heard?" I don't think so!

God says, "Hey! You can listen to what everybody else is saying today (which will change by this time tomorrow) or you can focus your thoughts on me and my Word…the Bible; the truth that will never change or pass away. You can follow the chattering of men and you'll end up like dried leaves being blown by the wind, not free, just out of control with no direction. Or, listen to me and you'll be like a beautiful tree down by the stream; drinking in the truth that, in the end, will set you truly free!"

———————————————————————

If any of you lacks wisdom, he should ask God, who gives generously to all without finding fault, and it will be given to him. James 1:5

PSALM 2

DEPENDENCE DAY

---

1 Why do the nations conspire and the peoples plot in vain? 2 The kings of the earth take their stand and the rulers gather together against the Lord and against his Anointed One. 3 "Let us break their chains," they say, "and throw off their fetters [or shackles for the feet]." 4 The One enthroned in heaven laughs; the Lord scoffs at them. 5 Then he rebukes them in his anger and terrifies them in his wrath, saying, 6 "I have installed my King on Zion, my holy hill." 7 I will proclaim the decree of the Lord: He said to me, "You are my Son; today I have become your Father. 8 Ask of me, and I will make the nations your inheritance, the ends of the earth your possession. 9 You will rule them with an iron scepter; you will dash them to pieces like pottery." 10 Therefore, you kings, be wise; be warned, you rulers of the earth. 11 Serve the Lord with fear and rejoice with trembling. 12 Kiss the Son, lest he be angry and you be destroyed in your way, for his wrath can flare up in a moment. Blessed are all who take refuge in him.

Have you ever been to the store and seen a screaming child being carted away by his parent? The kid is hollering, kicking and flailing, declaring, "I hate you! I hate you!" It soon becomes obvious that the parent has become pretty good at this. They're not embarrassed or intimidated by the scene their child is making. They're just quietly taking Johnny out to the parking lot for a little "time out" or perhaps a politically incorrect spanking!

4

Before we celebrate Johnny's demise too soon, you and I are just like him. Yep! We make our plans. We declare this and that as if we are in control. And then we sit proudly upon our iron horses as if to suggest, "I am in charge!" The worst of us join Frank Sinatra in a chorus of "I Did It My Way." Truth is, we are just being carried away by the ruthless hand of time and the ever-loving (but firm and just) arms of God. We can kick and scream as much as we like! We're going to the parking lot!

We boldly declare our independence from God and make up "the truth" as we think it ought to be. Then, we declare our "freedom" and cry out, "Let us break the chains!" as we ride away into the sunset. How romantic. Sadly, in an attempt to leave behind what we thought were God's chains to deprive us, we soon discover a whole new set of self-made irons, created by our ignorance and our so-called "freedom." And God; the One we took the stand against? He just smiles and carries us outside for a "time out" or better yet, a good spanking. (Last time I checked, God wasn't concerned with being politically correct.) You can go to the parking lot if you want. I've been there and it isn't any fun. Instead, I choose to serve the Lord and do it his way.

---

21 Once you were alienated from God and were enemies in your minds because of your evil behavior. 22 But now he has reconciled you by Christ's physical body through death to present you holy in his sight, without blemish and free from accusation. Colossians 1:21-22

PSALM 3

THE ROAR OF SILENCE

---

1 O Lord, how many are my foes! How many rise up against me! 2 Many are saying of me, "God will not deliver him." Selah 3 But you are a shield around me, O Lord; you bestow glory on me and lift up my head. 4 To the Lord I cry aloud, and he answers me from his holy hill. Selah 5 I lie down and sleep; I wake again, because the Lord sustains me. 6 I will not fear the tens of thousands drawn up against me on every side. 7 Arise, O Lord! Deliver me, O my God! Strike all my enemies on the jaw; break the teeth of the wicked. 8 From the Lord comes deliverance. May your blessing be on your people. Selah

King David had plenty of enemies. It comes with being a king. But in Psalm 3, his enemies are being led by his son Absolom. Can it get any worse than that? Your own son trying to kill you? But look what is at the end of verse two, just before David's rescue in verse three. It's the word "Selah" which means to take a "dramatic pause." (Stop! Think! Breathe! Listen!) And then David realizes, "**God is my shield!**"

When asked why they ride a motorcycle, many will say that it's their escape, a chance to think and put things in perspective. Just fifteen minutes of the wind in your face, the vibrations and the roar of an engine is enough for some people to get a whole new start on their day. Why?

Because it's so easy to be swallowed up by the Absoloms of this world. Life is coming at us so fast sometimes we lose our bearings. It's like riding through the fog and we have lost all sense of direction and perspective. We are no longer even sure of where we are. We need to rise above the mist. Selah. By pausing and listening for the voice of God.

If we would take the time to listen carefully, we would discover that we are not alone. We would realize like David that God Almighty is ready and willing to speak into our confusion and be our shield, protector and guide. He wants to put His hand under our chins and lift our heads so that we can see the truth. And what is the truth? It's that life is hard, but God is good and we don't have to go it alone. And it doesn't matter whether there are ten Absoloms or "tens of thousands" because in our corner we have God Almighty.

Take a ride with God today! Twist that throttle and celebrate the freedom you have in him. Take in all of creation; the mountains, the sky, the smell of fresh cut grass, and know that there is a God in Heaven who loves you very much! He is your shield and protector! Nobody cares more about you and your day than him! Selah.

---

27 My sheep listen to my voice; I know them, and they follow me. 28 I give them eternal life, and they shall never perish; no one can snatch them out of my hand. John 10:27-28

PSALM 4

SEARCHING IN ALL THE WRONG PLACES

---

1 Answer me when I call to you, O my righteous God. Give me relief from my distress; be merciful to me and hear my prayer. 2 How long, O men, will you turn my glory into shame? How long will you love delusions and seek false gods? Selah 3 Know that the Lord has set apart the godly for himself; the Lord will hear when I call to him. 4 In your anger do not sin; when you are on your beds, search your hearts and be silent. Selah 5 Offer right sacrifices and trust in the Lord. 6 Many are asking, "Who can show us any good?" Let the light of your face shine upon us, O Lord. 7 You have filled my heart with greater joy than when their grain and new wine abound. 8 I will lie down and sleep in peace, for you alone, O Lord, make me dwell in safety.

A casual grin on one side of his mouth reveals that Tim is somehow satisfied with himself as he signs on the bottom line with an animated slash and a dot. His newly purchased extra-dark sunglasses wrap around his face in an attempt to conceal his inner satisfaction, but somehow an air of confidence now surrounds him that anyone can see. He gets up from the desk as the salesman goes to finish the final paperwork. Meanwhile, in the clothing department, Tim carefully selects a minimal helmet, fingerless gloves and a leather vest with chains and conchos.

When Tim returns to the office with his new look he does so with an even more pronounced air of confidence - only now there is a swagger in his gait due to his new steel-toed engineer boots. (Did we mention that he was now an inch taller?) He shakes the salesman's hand one more time and exits the dealership to find his brand new motorcycle waiting for its first command. Tim throws a leg across the saddle as if he has done this hundreds of times before and glances over his shoulder to see if anyone has noticed. He stands the bike upright, grips the clutch, starts the motor and roars away. But he hasn't proceeded more than a hundred feet when he finds himself and his new chromed stallion horizontal in the bushes. What was created in Tim's mind over the last few months has now vanished in an instant and all of the leather and chrome in the world will not restore his sense of self-generated confidence and dignity. **"How long, O men, will you love delusions and seek false gods?"**

Motorcycles are cool - very cool! They're fun to ride and can be better for the soul than a year of therapy. They are not, however, metallic gods or miracle workers that will make all of your problems go away or change in an instant who you have become through the years. Every one of us is just a man or a woman, in all of our vulnerability, riding a machine. You are not bigger, better, stronger, sexier or wiser because you ride. Tim had a delusion that a new motorcycle would make him something that he was not. In one embarrassing moment, he was once again just plain Tim. He gathered up what was left of his bruised self-image and wandered off, once again in search of lasting answers.

We often find ourselves in a place where we cry out to God, begging Him to send help because we have depleted all of our own resources and have nowhere else to turn. We have tried everything and done it all! We've explored the bottom of many a beer and scaled the heights of our corporate ladders in search of the truth. We've bought "stuff", got religion, changed jobs, and maybe even spouses in hope of finding something of lasting value. But everything tangible on Earth has failed us and we sense that if there is an answer, maybe heaven has it.

So since we feel free to petition God in our moments of frustration and despair, he has every right to then question us. As we beg for his mercy, God is wondering why we have neglected an ongoing relationship with him and chosen to use him like a rich relative that we suddenly seek to know when we learn that they have won the lottery. Relationships are best built over time, over coffee, long walks and honest talks. Answers rarely come in a moment, but develop over a lifetime. Unanswered questions aren't nearly as frightening when you walk with someone who has been on the other side and is not afraid.

When we have a relationship with God we are urged to listen intently on our beds at night and to trust in him for all that we need and for all we want to become. The result of this is sheer joy rising up and filling us with hope because now the answers are coming from someone who knows rather than one who wanders in desperation. Sweet peace and restful sleep are the fruit not of delusions, but of visions.

11 For no one can lay any foundation other than the one already laid, which is Jesus Christ. 12 If any man builds on this foundation using gold, silver, costly stones, wood, hay or straw, 13 his work will be shown for what it is, because the Day will bring it to light. It will be revealed with fire, and the fire will test the quality of each man's work. **I Corinthians 3: 11-13**

PSALM 5

DID YOU GAS UP THIS MORNING?

1 Give ear to my words, O Lord, consider my sighing. 2 Listen to my cry for help, my King and my God, for to you I pray. 3 In the morning, O Lord, you hear my voice; in the morning I lay my requests before you and wait in expectation.

11 But let all who take refuge in you be glad; let them ever sing for joy. Spread your protection over them, that those who love your name may rejoice in you. 12 For surely, O Lord, you bless the righteous; you surround them with your favor as with a shield.

I can't think of a bad time of day to ride; morning, afternoon or evening. Each has its benefits. But one of the best things about a cross-country trip is the promise of a new morning each day. Living in Southern California, the annual trek to Sturgis is no afternoon scoot. It needs to be a well thought through and planned adventure. Some wince at the 1600 miles one way, but if every day is truly a new day, then Sturgis is just four or five hundred miles…one day at a time.

With every morning, the bones have recovered, the tanks have been filled and the heart is recharged with expectation. We have prepared for the day by feeding our bodies, fueling our machines and studying the maps, choosing the best route for everything that we want to see and do. (NOTE: Don't be surprised if near the end of the trip the daily routes are chosen according to the shortest distance rather than sight seeing opportunities!)

So it is with prayer. It's a new day...a fresh start...a new set of opportunities. We need to feed our spirits, fuel our minds and study God's Word in order to set a course for the day. **"In the morning, O Lord, you hear my voice; in the morning I lay my requests before you and wait in expectation."** Why wait for the middle of the afternoon to seek God? Why wait until the phones are ringing and the kids are crying and the world demands our attention?

Someday in the near future, get up early and take a solo ride on your bike. Meander down your favorite country road, through a nearby canyon or along the oceanfront. Breathe the fresh air and invite the Spirit of God to ride with you. Seek him in the early morning when everything is fresh and new.

Having done this, God encourages us to be glad because we have chosen him as our first refuge and declined to rely upon ourselves. **"Spread your protection over them"** is what the writer prays for those who seek God. He then tells us to **"sing for joy!"** Go ahead! No one can hear you over the roar of your engine. Break out in a song that celebrates your God and his goodness and his protection over you. He is absolutely able and qualified to take care of you and your needs. Trust in him!

Very early in the morning, while it was still dark, Jesus got up, left the house and went off to a solitary place, where he prayed. Mark 1:35

PSALM 6

Have Mercy!

---

1 O Lord, do not rebuke me in your anger or discipline me in your wrath. 2 Be merciful to me, Lord, for I am faint; O Lord, heal me, for my bones are in agony. 3 My soul is in anguish. How long, O Lord, how long? 4 Turn, O Lord, and deliver me; save me because of your unfailing love.

9 The Lord has heard my cry for mercy; the Lord accepts my prayer. 10 All my enemies will be ashamed and dismayed; they will turn back in sudden disgrace.

The usual crew was sitting around the proverbial "pickle barrel" at the local motorcycle dealership, exchanging horror stories from the road. "She turned right in front of me - RIGHT IN FRONT OF ME! I didn't have a chance." Another interrupts, "It's a good thing that I slowed down before going through that intersection. I mean, the light was green, but something told me to slow down. Sure as I did, here comes this kid in one of those lowered Japanese racers... and on a cell phone no less. I was clearly in the right, but I could have been creamed!"

Sid tells of the injustice of being cited for excessively loud pipes by an overly zealous rookie cop. "I do the speed limit and I obey all the laws. I even wear a DOT approved helmet, but on the wrong day in the wrong upscale neighborhood I get a ticket for what the police say were

16

'excessively loud pipes!' How did he know how loud they were? He didn't have a decibel meter!" And the stories continued throughout the morning about how mistreated we all were and how unjust the world was. "**How long, O Lord, how long?"**

How many times have you heard someone declare (or maybe even you yourself), "I only want what's fair." Or, "What we really need here is justice…just give me justice!" Probably more than a few times with today's entitlement minded society. But the writer of this Psalm has a more realistic understanding of his situation.

Instead of demanding justice and seeking his rights, he cries out to the Lord to have mercy upon him. And truth be told, that's what we all really need - MERCY! Sure, I complain about the time when I was unjustly treated but how many times did I get away with running that "yellow" light or rolling that stop sign? If we received our demand for justice and truly got what was coming to us, we would all end up as grease spots on the carpet for we are all guilty of breaking every one of God's laws.

But instead of giving us what's coming to us, our loving heavenly Father wisely sees through our rantings and tantrums and instead gives us his mercy. So we would be wise to shut-up and gladly receive mercy over justice. He is happy to provide it if we ask sincerely. Don't try to hide your feelings and failures from God….nothing surprises him. Be honest and rest assured that we will be heard and he will answer our cry.

3 All of us also lived among them at one time, gratifying the cravings of our sinful nature and following its desires and thoughts. Like the rest, we were by nature objects of wrath. 4 But because of his great love for us, God, who is rich in mercy, 5 made us alive with Christ even when we were dead in transgressions--it is by grace you have been saved. Ephesians 2:3-5

PSALM 7

MY OWN WORST ENEMY

---

1 O Lord my God, I take refuge in you; save and deliver me from all who pursue me, 2 or they will tear me like a lion and rip me to pieces with no one to rescue me. 3 O Lord my God, if I have done this and there is guilt on my hands --- 4 if I have done evil to him who is at peace with me or without cause have robbed my foe --- 5 then let my enemy pursue and overtake me; let him trample my life to the ground and make me sleep in the dust. Selah

14 He who is pregnant with evil and conceives trouble gives birth to disillusionment. 15 He who digs a hole and scoops it out falls into the pit he has made.

We were preparing to go on a ride with a large group and were just about to finish up the pre-ride meeting. We carefully explained about "tanks full and bladders empty" and reviewed all of the usual hand signals for slowing down, debris in the road and emergencies. One rider in the back raised his hand and said, "Don't forget this one!" He then began to tap the top of his helmet with the palm of his glove. This, as many experienced riders will know, is the sign for "law enforcement ahead" (palm on the helmet indicating the bubble gum machine on top of most older police cars). I suggested to the contributor that this sign would not be necessary since we had no intentions of exceeding the speed limit or chasing children through the park.

The funny thing is, the guy who would warn us of police would probably be the first to complain if he were to get a ticket. Truth be told, we are usually our own worst problem. "I got a ticket!" says one rider, but he left out the fact that he had chosen to speed. Another complains, "I had an accident and the cops roughed me up!", but fails to mention that his blood alcohol was twice the legal limit causing him to be a handful.

This line of thinking is not limited to the motorcycle world. One lonely person moans, "I don't have any friends!", but they have never invested the time to be a friend to someone else. A bitter forty-something complains, "My spouse dumped me!" but neglects to mention that he had been distant with his partner and flirtatious with others. "My life is in ruins!" you say, but have you ever taken God's Word seriously in what it has to say about life and living? **"He who is pregnant with evil and conceives trouble gives birth to disillusionment. He who digs a hole and scoops it out falls into the pit he has made."** One writer put it this way, "I have seen the enemy and it is me."

Why are we so much like the man who has Limburger cheese on his moustache but complains that the whole world stinks? Why are we so blind to our own contributions to our dysfunctional lives? Why are we so disillusioned about the truth? God has given us a road map for life and most have chosen to ignore or disobey it. The New Testament says it like this: **"Do not be deceived: God cannot be mocked. A man reaps what he sows. The one who sows** to please his sinful nature, from that nature will reap destruction; the one who sows to please the Spirit, from the Spirit will reap eternal life." (Galatians 6:7-8)

I know who I am. That's why I cry "mercy" instead of "justice." Justice would be the end of me while mercy is a loving God giving me a new day and another chance to do it right. And from this point forward, I choose to plant seeds that won't grow up to be man-eating plants!

Flee the evil desires of youth, and pursue righteousness, faith, love and peace, along with those who call on the Lord out of a pure heart.   2Timothy 2:22

PSALM 8

ROLLING AMBASSADORS

---

1 O Lord, our Lord, how majestic is your name in all the earth! You have set your glory above the heavens. 2 From the lips of children and infants you have ordained praise because of your enemies, to silence the foe and the avenger. 3 When I consider your heavens, the work of your fingers, the moon and the stars, which you have set in place, 4 what is man that you are mindful of him, the son of man that you care for him? 5 You made him a little lower than the heavenly beings and crowned him with glory and honor. 6 You made him ruler over the works of your hands; you put everything under his feet: 7 all flocks and herds and the beasts of the field, 8 the birds of the air, and the fish of the sea, all that swim the paths of the seas. 9 O Lord, our Lord, how majestic is your name in all the earth!

When I think of the word majestic, my mind immediately envisions riding through Yosemite or Zion national park. The dictionary defines majestic as "very grand or dignified; lofty or stately." These beautiful rock formations seem to qualify as they captivate our eyes and draw them upwards towards the heavens…towards God.

The popular word used today might be "awesome." But we hear almost everything referred to as awesome: awesome pipes, awesome paint job, awesome ride, awesome wind and awesome band. None of these things even comes close to what the writer of this psalm has in mind when he speaks of the majesty of our God who created all of the

great sights, smells, sounds and beautiful scenery that we are so fortunate to be part of as we ride. Isn't that one of the greatest things about riding a motorcycle, having all five senses invaded by creation?

The cliffs tower hundreds of feet above us. The rock formations are so beautiful they defy description. Barren rocks graced with crystal falls that spill over the side and splash below dare us to deny that there is a maker. And yet, with all of this beauty and grandeur, too expansive and breathtaking to do justice with mere words or even fully capture in a photograph, man is the focus of God's special favor.

We are told that God thinks about us and cares for us as he considers our individual needs. Just as the beautiful landscape, we are created to reflect his glory and honor as we have been placed as caretakers over his creation. All of creation, including man, has been designed to point to the greatness of God. Talk about awesome! What a responsibility...to model the nature and character of our Creator to a clueless and indifferent world. As God is full of mercy, we are to be full of mercy. As God is full of kindness, joy, forgiveness and love, we are to be the same way towards each other. And as people go through life and interact with us, they should go away having a sense of the presence of God. We bear his fruit...so the world can taste his sweetness.

In the same way, let your light shine before men, that they may see your good deeds and praise your Father in heaven. Matthew 5:16

PSALM 9 2/21/13

MOTORCYCLE FANATIC

---

*1 I will praise you, O Lord, with all my heart; I will tell of
your wonders. 2 I will be glad and rejoice in you; I will sing
praise to your name, O Most High.*

Remember your first bike? Wasn't it a beauty? Even if
it was an old Honda trail 90, I'll bet it was pretty special
to you! Did you hide it under a sheet in the garage or did
you parade it all over town? We were so excited about
our first Harley that we took pictures of it while it was
still at the dealership. Later we would have a professional
photographer take our portrait on the bike. Just like a
newborn baby we would show our pictures to all of our
friends and relatives. And when we took our first trip
to Sturgis, all of the snapshots had to have the bike in
the foreground. "Here's Mount Rushmore - and our
Harley!" and, "Here's the entrance to the Badlands - and
our Harley!" Why did we do that? Because owning that
bike gave us a sense of pride and we were eager to share all
of the good times with others.

Some people are sports fans while others are fans of
movie stars and rock and roll legends. We wear their
shirts and hang their posters on our walls. (I've always
loved the six guys who show up topless in a frozen football
stadium with their pro team's name spelled out across

their naked hairy chests!) Sometimes we are referred to as "motorcycle enthusiasts." Either way, we're "fans" which is an abbreviation of the word "fanatic." David (the writer of Psalm 9) was a fan of God and he vowed, "I will tell of all your wonders." According to this Psalm, God had defeated David's enemies and been an agent of justice and righteousness. He was a "refuge" for David and for all the oppressed. The promise is, "Those who know your name will trust in you, for you, Lord, have never forsaken those who seek you." (v10)

Funny thing about people, we are told by retail experts that if someone is happy with a product they will tell three people, but if they are unhappy with a product they will tell ten. Why is that? Perhaps because human nature takes for granted those good things that have come into their lives. And even though we know that God has blessed us, we fear the label "fanatic!" Oh, we'll stand up and scream at a concert or a football game. Some will even don painted faces and wigs to express their enthusiasm for their favorite team, but say a good word about God in public....the one who makes all of life possible? That would be fanatical! Suddenly we become shy, at a loss for words and scared! Big tough bikers who declare that they would give their life for a brother suddenly become terrified or even ashamed to speak one good word for their God. Not David! He's bold and enthusiastic...a real fanatic when he declares, "Sing praises to the Lord...proclaim among the nations what he has done."

Motorcycles and movie stars come and go but God is forever! If you'll be such a fanatic as to tattoo the name of your favorite motorcycle onto your body can't you tell somebody about the great things God has done in your life? C'mon! Speak up! Be a little fanatical for God!

I am not ashamed of the Gospel, because it is the power of God for the salvation of everyone who believes. **Romans 1:16**

PSALM 10

BUSTED! YOU'RE ON CANDID CAMERA

1 Why, O Lord, do you stand far off? Why do you hide yourself in times of trouble? 2 In his arrogance the wicked man hunts down the weak, who are caught in the schemes he devises. 3 He boasts of the cravings of his heart; he blesses the greedy and reviles the Lord. 4 In his pride the wicked does not seek him; in all his thoughts there is no room for God. 5 His ways are always prosperous; he is haughty and your laws are far from him; he sneers at all his enemies. 6 He says to himself, "Nothing will shake me; I'll always be happy and never have trouble."

14 But you, O God, do see trouble and grief; you consider it to take it in hand. The victim commits himself to you; you are the helper of the fatherless.

Ever since I started riding motorcycles I have been increasingly aware of drivers who brazenly ignore the law. I have had several friends who have fallen victim to the one who runs the "yellow" light or rolls the stop sign. Too many have been injured or killed by those who drive with reckless abandon saying in essence, "The laws do not apply to me."

A yellow light used to mean caution and prepare to stop. Now it means "speed up" and get to work one minute earlier. In stark resistance to this cultural anarchy, I have determined to stop for yellow lights, drive the speed limit and get there when I get there.

One day as I was riding through town, I pulled into the left hand turn lane of an intersection and stopped first in line as the light turned yellow. Behind me, the driver of a small pick-up seemed restless and after stopping briefly, he pulled out of line and maneuvered around me to make a left hand turn through an already red light. I couldn't believe what I was seeing. This amounted to nothing less than brazen disrespect for the traffic laws and the lives of others! This driver was thumbing his nose at authority and declaring, "Rules don't apply to me…. I'll do as I please and if it endangers others then so be it." Outraged by this display of lawlessness, I wondered, "Where are the cops when you need them?"

Psalm ten asks a similar question about God. It is an ancient human dilemma…the prosperity of the wicked while the righteous are allowed to suffer. And the world asks, "Does God see?" "If he sees does he care?" As if that were not enough, as they persistently practice evil and get off scot-free, lawless people grow more bold as they perceive there to be no consequences to their behavior. We are told in essence that they are lulled into a sense of complacency assuming that God will never call them to accountability.

But herein lies a serious misunderstanding because we confuse God's patience with what seems to be an indifference towards justice. Not at all! Verse 14 assures us that God does indeed notice the lawlessness, the sin and the pain and grief it can cause others. We are assured that he will deal with it and is indeed a helper of the victim, the oppressed and the fatherless. Do you see a gross lack of justice? Appeal to God and allow him to encourage you and take up your cause. God is faithful and decisively acts to protect the oppressed.

And so, evil goes on seemingly unchecked until one day, unexpected, a pricey traffic ticket arrives in the mail courtesy of an unseen intersection surveillance camera which is always running. Busted! You're on Candid Camera.

Do not be deceived: God cannot be mocked. A man reaps what he sows. **Galatians 6:7**

PSALM 11

No More Running

1 In the Lord I take refuge. How can you say to me: "Flee like a bird to your mountain. 2 For look, the wicked bend their bows; they set their arrows against the strings to shoot from the shadows at the upright in heart. 3 When the foundations are being destroyed, what can the righteous do?" 4 The Lord is in his holy temple; the Lord is on his heavenly throne.

Everybody has a mountain, meaning a safe place, a retreat, a manmade source of protection and security. It is a place they consider to be higher ground; elevated and protected from the floods of life below. It is usually their first line of defense; the first place they go when something sounds the alarm.

In the days of old, higher ground always made the best defensive position. From there, a soldier had a better view, his weapons were more effective and his enemies were forced to fight an uphill battle. Today's mountains may vary according to one's resources. The rich man's mountain is his wealth and influence. The strong man's mountain may be his strength and ability to intimidate. Even addictions can be a form of defense against a perceived enemy. At best, however, these "mountains" are still only manmade and therefore far from true security.

My wife and I were riding along the Northern California coast and it had been raining off and on all day. We were cold and hungry and just a few miles south of Fort Bragg, eager to arrive and get a room for the night. The little town seemed busier than one might expect for its size. The streets and restaurants were full …and so were all of the motels! Unbeknownst to us, there was a statewide youth soccer championship being held there that weekend. The place was crawling with kids, mothers and SUV's.

It was fifty miles to the next town, getting dark and now it was beginning to rain pretty steadily. I was so cold as I approached a motel parking lot that as I put my foot down, my half frozen, stiff leg hesitated for a moment and I almost dropped the bike. As my wife and I sat staring at the "No Vacancy" sign which flashed without mercy, we pondered what to do. (It was the third motel we had stopped at since being in town.) Perhaps we could offer to pay double the rate or volunteer to sleep in the lobby. We even considered spending the night drinking endless cups of coffee at Denny's or attempting to negotiate a night at the police station. But alas, these were only our man-made "mountain retreats." Instead, we sat there at the end of our rope and we simply prayed, "God, please help us! We need a refuge, a shelter and a place to sleep." I must admit that my faith was tiny as I walked into the motel lobby. (The hum of the flashing sign seemed to mock me as I approached the door.) The night manager was on the phone, so I waited more out of fatigue than patience. When he hung up the phone, I asked if there might be a room available. To my complete surprise he answered, "You're the luckiest man on the North Coast tonight. There are no rooms available for 200 miles but that phone call was a last minute cancellation. How many of you will there be?"

Luck had nothing to do with it! I knew that and I told him so. Prayer opened the way for God to bless his children. Never has a hot bath felt so good. Outside, the cold rain was coming down and we were inside wrapped in warm blankets. In the Lord we found refuge. There is never a need to run to the mountains when our help and salvation is also our best friend.

In this Psalm, King David finds himself under attack. (That's the way it goes with kings I suppose!) But as David's friends and advisors are telling him to run for the hills, David says, "No, I take refuge in the Lord. He is my only defense." The alarm has sounded and the enemy has the king in his sites and defeat looks imminent! So what is a righteous man to do? He can remember that God is STILL in control! He can choose NOT to trust in his own strengths, but get on his knees and fight like a man. David may have devised a plan and he may have mustered his armies, but FIRST he went to prayer and focused on his God through worship. Prayer is NOT our last resort. It is our first privilege and only reliable higher ground!

Jesus said, "Come to me, all you who are weary and burdened, and I will give you rest." Matthew 11:28

PSALM 12

THE MALIGNANT TONGUE

---

1 Help, Lord, for the godly are no more; the faithful have vanished from among men. 2 Everyone lies to his neighbor; their flattering lips speak with deception. 3 May the Lord cut off all flattering lips and every boastful tongue 4 that says, "We will triumph with our tongues; we own our lips - who is our master?" 5 "Because of the oppression of the weak and the groaning of the needy, I will now arise," says the Lord. "I will protect them from those who malign them." 6 And the words of the Lord are flawless, like silver refined in a furnace of clay, purified seven times. 7 O Lord, you will keep us safe and protect us from such people forever. 8 The wicked freely strut about when what is vile is honored among men.

Laughlin, Nevada - April 2002. The papers read, "Rival motorcycle gangs clashed in a southern Nevada casino early Saturday, leaving three men dead, at least 13 other people wounded and -- for a few hours -- an entire town on lockdown. Police characterized the melee at Harrah's Laughlin Casino as the worst shooting incident in the history of Nevada casinos."

Earlier in the week and in previous years, the Laughlin River Run was an escape for otherwise hard-working middle class people. It's hard to imagine, however, a respected first grade teacher from L.A. now riding topless down the boulevard or a corporate CEO encouraging her to "take it all off." Did local law enforcement and casino personnel suddenly find themselves overwhelmed by the sheer numbers of tens of thousands of visitors gone wild, or did the dynamics of the crowd slowly sneak up on everybody over the years and erode basic morality and common sense?

Like those of you reading this story, we've been to a lot of motorcycle events. They are all a little crazy, but the Laughlin River Run had become increasingly "nuts" each year and in 2002 the stage was set for just about anything to happen. An atmosphere of abandonment started with a little drinking...a little nudity...a little violence and then an all out shooting. Some would argue that one has little to do with the other, but Psalm 12:8 tells us that when that which is "vile" (morally base or evil; wicked; depraved; sinful) is honored and accepted by men, it sets the acceptance for an even greater wickedness to NOT only sneak around in the shadows, but "freely strut about."

The author of this Psalm writes as if he lived among us today and understands the conditions of our time. "Where are the godly...where are the faithful?" And the world responds, "We will do and say what we please! Nobody will tell us what to do!" And God says, "I will rise up and respond to those who have fallen victim to the wicked." What are we to think? Is there a day of judgment coming? Will God "balance the books" one day? We are sure of it because our God makes no threats - only promises. His words are pure and flawless - what He says is true! The "wicked freely strut about" for now - but a day of reckoning is coming. God will not overlook vile behavior left unchecked or winked at.

"Vile" behavior, however, is not limited to murder and mayhem. Vile behavior can begin with something as small as the tongue. There are at least five references to verbal sins; lies, flattering lips, deception, boasting and maligning which is to speak evil about someone. In fact, the word malign is the root of the word malignant, which speaks of a wildly growing cancerous tumor. What better description could we have of the damage that is done daily by the tongues of men?

Contrast the malignant tongue with the "flawless" words of God which are described as, "silver refined in a furnace, purified seven times." How will our tongues govern our lives this day? Will they be instruments of destruction or mercy? Will they wound or will they heal? Are they purified by God's Spirit or tainted with ulterior motives? God vows to protect those who have been maligned. On which side of righteousness will you be found?

---

5 Likewise the tongue is a small part of the body, but it makes great boasts. Consider what a great forest is set on fire by a small spark. 6 The tongue also is a fire, a world of evil among the parts of the body. It corrupts the whole person, sets the whole course of his life on fire, and is itself set on fire by hell. James 3:5-6

PSALM 13

WAITING FOR GOD ON THE SIDE OF THE ROAD

1 How long, O lord? Will you forget me forever? How long will you hide your face from me? 2 How long must I wrestle with my thoughts and every day have sorrow in my heart? How long will my enemy triumph over me? 3 Look on me and answer, O Lord my God. Give light to my eyes, or I will sleep in death; 4 my enemy will say, "I have overcome him," and my foes will rejoice when I fall. 5 But I trust in your unfailing love; my heart rejoices in your salvation. 6 I will sing to the Lord, for he has been good to me.

I ran out of gas today! On the older Harley evolutions, there is no gas gauge. When filling it up, one must remember to reset the tripometer in order to anticipate when it is time to gas up again. What I thought was a full tank surprised me when my bike sputtered and choked its way to a stop on the side of the road. It was a well-traveled street at rush hour and so I waited patiently, thinking someone would surely stop and offer help. People waved and honked; some even gave me the thumbs up and nodded with a smile, but no one bothered to ask why I was standing on the side of the road next to a lifeless Harley. Several riders even broke the golden rule and failed to come to the aide of a fellow biker.

Sometimes we get the feeling that's the way it is with God. We are stuck in a bad situation. Life has dealt us a losing hand or else we have created a mess and gotten ourselves in a fix like I did when I chose not to fill up my tank when it occurred to me earlier in the week. Either way, we need help because without it we are going nowhere. Life passes us by, people smile and wave and ask how we are without really wanting to know any of the particulars. All the while we are in a bad situation and we know it.

Not only does it seem that no one cares, but we become skeptical about even God being aware. Worse yet, since he is supposed to know everything, he must be aware of my situation and since he can do anything, he could certainly fix this. We wrestle with these thoughts assured that we have a loving God but are seemingly left in a quagmire. At this point, our enemy Satan is more than happy to help fuel the fire of doubt and discredit God: "Gee! He must not care about you!" Suddenly we feel alone and vulnerable. The world is unkind and adversarial and the odds are stacked against us. We imagine that when we go down for the count there is going to be a huge party to celebrate our demise!

But in verse five the writer chooses not to dwell on human understanding but instead focuses on God and trusts him for a timely rescue. He believes that God will not turn a deaf ear and even anticipates and knows our needs before we cry out to him. God doesn't honk and he may not even wave, but our roadside experience tells us that our Father in Heaven always stops for those who are waiting on him. That does not mean that everything will always work out the way we would like it to, but it does mean that we are never alone in our circumstances. Even if a friendly biker doesn't have a spare gallon of gas, he'll stay with you until someone who does comes along. Trust in God!

...for your Father knows what you need before you ask him.
Matthew 6:8

PSALM 14

RIDING LIKE A FOOL

---

1 The fool says in his heart, "There is no God." They are corrupt, their deeds are vile; there is no one who does good. 2 The Lord looks down from heaven on the sons of men to see if there are any who understand, any who seek God. 3 All have turned aside, they have together become corrupt; there is no one who does good, not even one. 4 Will evildoers never learn - those who devour my people as men eat bread and who do not call on the Lord? 5 There they are, overwhelmed with dread, for God is present in the company of the righteous.

I was sitting at an outdoor lunch bar one day, wearing my motorcycle colors. Included in the embroidery on my back were the words, "Jesus Is Lord." I was content to sit there alone, munching on my burger when a voice from behind me asked with a sneer, "I see that you are a Christian. Do you really believe that @*!!?"

We hear a lot about atheists, but it isn't every day that you actually get to meet one. An atheist is someone who doesn't believe in God - but I've never believed in atheists. I've always thought that somewhere down inside of every atheist there must still be a flicker of faith. Few would loudly voice their opinion in the company of a large group that there is no God. Most kids went to Sunday school or vacation Bible school at some point in their lives. Everybody knows SOMETHING about Noah, David and Goliath and Jesus! Most have heard that Jesus was one of the good guys who fed the hungry and healed the sick. Nevertheless, here is this guy interrupting my lunch.

As I turned around I saw an aged biker standing with the sun at his back, making it difficult to make out the details of his face. He stood there waiting for an answer; "Do you really believe that stuff?" After I assured him that I did we talked for about half an hour and when all was said that was going to be said I, for the first time in my life, believed that I had actually met an atheist. It left me cold and nervous for him as he mounted his café racer and headed out for the open highway. "Vaya con Dios!" didn't seem to be an appropriate farewell since he wasn't "going with God"- he was just going.

There are far more agnostics than atheists in the world because it is much more comfortable to say "I don't know if there is a god" than to burn the bridges of hope altogether. While most will not declare their atheism, the heart's disbelief soon gives way to deeds and actions that speak far louder than mere words. On their beds alone at night, sleep eludes them as they find themselves overwhelmed with guilt, anxiety and dread because they can sense that something is missing from their lives and their hopes are built on shaky ground. God is not a part of their foundation.

Have you found yourself thinking that God isn't there, doesn't care or isn't watching? Don't fall into the trap of being what Psalm 14 terms "a fool." Denying God's existence opens the way for moral indifference and deficiency. Right on the heals of this are actions that lack integrity and decision making that is corrupt. The Spirit of God is the moral light and compass of this world. Without Him, we are left directionless and in the dark.

Let the existence of God sink deep into your heart. Believe that he loves you and that you are his child. Begin to return that love through prayer and worship. Then you can know, like the writer of this Psalm, that he is your refuge, your God and your best friend.

34b For out of the overflow of the heart the mouth speaks. 35 The good man brings good things out of the good stored up in him, and the evil man brings evil things out of the evil stored up in him. Matthew 12:34b-35

PSALM 15

ROAD CONDITIONS

1 Lord, who may dwell in your sanctuary? Who may live on your holy hill? 2 He whose walk is blameless and who does what is righteous, who speaks the truth from his heart 3 and has no slander on his tongue, who does his neighbor no wrong and casts no slur on his fellowman, 4 who despises a vile man but honors those who fear the Lord, who keeps his oath even when it hurts, 5 who lends his money without usury and does not accept a bribe against the innocent. He who does these things will never be shaken.

I remember riding down the road one sunny afternoon... taking the side roads, skirting around the busy freeways and wandering through some beautiful backcountry. My wife and I were approaching a stop light at a busy intersection when we hit an unseen patch of oil. In a split second I could feel the loss of traction to the rear tire as it slid sideways. As suddenly as it had happened, it was over and we were once again on dry pavement.

I know what is expected of me and my machine when riding on normal surfaces. However, things like water, sand and oil make for more unpredictable circumstances. We all want to know what the rules and expectations are in any given situation. In this Psalm, David is asking God, "What kind of a man is it who can live in your presence enjoying your safety and protection?" God's answer is short and to the point.

It's not a lengthy list of rules. It doesn't mention taking away our fun and it doesn't include attending any particular church. God's list has nothing to do with those things but focuses solely on the condition of a person's heart. But though the list may be concise, it's still an impossibility for me in my humanness. On the contrary, I mess up regularly and I don't always do what is right. I sometimes don't tell the truth...especially to myself and sometimes I cannot resist saying something unkind about someone else.

But that is precisely why God sent his son Jesus because he knew we could never hope to live a life that would allow us to spend an eternity with him. We need a savior to rescue us from ourselves and give us clean hands and a pure heart. The righteousness of Jesus has been assigned to us so when we stand before God, he sees the purity and integrity of his son and not the fact that we are sinners.

This is Good News because then we can live under God's protection. We're never going to be perfect this side of heaven. We will still make wrong choices from time to time. We may encounter a few oil slicks or a patch of gravel but like the bike, our lives will soon grab dry pavement and once again be on track. We won't be going down!

---

21 But now a righteousness from God, apart from law, has been made known, to which the Law and the Prophets testify. 22 This righteousness from God comes through faith in Jesus Christ to all who believe. Romans 3:21-22

PSALM 16

SHINY NEW BIKE

---

1 Keep me safe, O God, for in you I take refuge. 2 I said to the Lord, "You are my Lord; apart from you I have no good thing."

4 The sorrows of those will increase who run after other gods. I will not pour out their libations [or sacrifices] of blood or take up their names on my lips. 5 Lord, you have assigned me my portion and my cup; you have made my lot secure. 6 The boundary lines have fallen for me in pleasant places; surely I have a delightful inheritance.

Stop by the local motorcycle shop on any weekend and the chances are good that you will meet a few friends eye-balling all the new bikes for sale. Casual conversation usually gets around to the immediate or inevitable need for a new bike. Everyone nods approvingly as if they understand completely why this acquisition is essential.... an unquestionable necessity. The truth is, anything that we desire in our affluent western culture is usually not very difficult to justify. We see it...we want it...we buy it...any way we can!

Now, every rider will need a new bike sooner or later. Engines wear out and colors fade. But the constant drooling and sleepless nights thinking about chrome and paint jobs betrays that something is missing within and qualifies us as a candidate for idolatry. But you protest,

"I couldn't be guilty of idolatry! I'm an American! I don't have any statues with fat bellies and I don't keep any shrines in my back yard!" But make no mistake, idolatry is more basic than this. Idolatry, in any form, is the artificial and impotent substitute for the real thing. When people are empty on the inside, they go looking for something that satisfies. It may be money, an affair, chrome or even chocolate...ANYTHING that might fill the void. But GOD is the only shape that fits in this hole and apart from him we have nothing that is truly good!

The Psalmist resolves to steadfastly resist the urge to let anything but God fill his emptiness. Instead, in verses 5-6, the writer speaks to the value of contentment as he lets God give him what he needs instead of him scrambling for everything he wants. We can then rest knowing that what God has assigned us is truly the best. If you need a new bike, buy a new bike, but don't be fooled into thinking that a bright and shiny new toy will ever fill an empty heart, especially if we can't afford it or it brings distress into our relationships.

The boundary lines spoken of in verse six speak to the inheritance that we are allotted as a child of God. As we rest with contentment in the place he has provided for us, we can be thankful that what he gives us is truly good in every respect. Need a new job or a new bike or a whole new life? Maybe...but perhaps seeking the Lord FIRST is the best answer.

Jesus said, "But seek first his kingdom and his righteousness, and all these things will be given to you as well." Matthew 6:33

PSALM 17

CONFESSIONS OF A GUTTER MOUTH

---

1 Hear, O Lord, my righteous plea; listen to my cry. Give ear to my prayer—it does not rise from deceitful lips. 2 May my vindication come from you; may your eyes see what is right. 3 Though you probe my heart and examine me at night, though you test me, you will find nothing; I have resolved that my mouth will not sin. 4 As for the deeds of men -- by the word of your lips I have kept myself from the ways of the violent. 5 My steps have held to your paths; my feet have not slipped. 6 I call on you, O God, for you will answer me; give ear to me and hear my prayer. 7 Show the wonder of your great love, you who save by your right hand those who take refuge in you from their foes. 8 Keep me as the apple of your eye; hide me in the shadow of your wings…"

I've changed a lot since I started riding a Harley. Some of the changes were on purpose, like the practical necessity of wearing blue jeans and boots almost everywhere I go. One summer of rallies and poker runs left my closet full of nothing but black tee shirts - not white, not brown and not blue, but BLACK! Some of the changes I went looking for. I wanted "the look" and so within the first year I had shaved my head, grown a goatee, pierced my ears and braved a few tattoos. My new persona was emerging - even though I knew I was still just a RUB (Rich Urban Biker). But not all of the changes were on purpose or welcomed.

My private thoughts were challenged and I found that I had to be careful where my eyes lingered. There is no shortage of flesh and cleavage at bike rallies. Skin is in and looking straight ahead is sometimes an exercise in self-discipline. Not only were my eyes under siege, my ears weighed heavy under the burden of constant vulgarity. Not just "bad" words here and there, but an assault of vile verbiage and stories, one right after another; cursing men, degrading women and mocking God's name. And if it wasn't coming in through my ears it was coming in through my eyes as I read the back of a sweaty tee shirt.

Now don't get me wrong - I'm no prude! I went to junior high and high school with everyone else. Anyone can smash their thumb with a hammer and let out an expletive. That's not what I'm talking about here. If you've been riding for any length of time, you know what I'm referring to. It's a forced march that drives us through rivers of raw verbal sewage, leaving one feeling the need for a hot shower at the end of the experience. And as stinky and messy as it is - vulgarity is also contagious. It begins when someone cuts you off on the freeway and you say something that you didn't mean to - and you regret it. It shows up again a week later only this time you justify your choice of words without regret. Pretty soon, words that had not peppered your vocabulary since your youth begin to now flow freely between your ears and too often, out of your pie hole. And then you realize - you've changed. You've become a gutter mouth.

Why is this such a big deal? They're just words right? Wrong! First of all foul language betrays our ignorance and lack of creative speech. Any idiot can cuss. Secondly, the words can be incredibly dishonoring of others and not at all what we really mean in our hearts. When I hear someone tell another to "Go to hell," I know that they would never say such a thing if they understood what hell was really like. Thirdly, such language robs us of the immediate presence and power of God's Spirit. The scripture tells us to **"Pray without ceasing."** How can we do this if our mouths are filled with profanity? The scripture also implores us, **"Finally, brothers, whatever is true, whatever is noble, whatever is right, whatever is pure, whatever is lovely, whatever is admirable—if anything is excellent or praiseworthy—think about such things."** How can this happen once we have surrendered our tongues to a far inferior vocabulary of ugliness, the very opposite of what scripture demands of us?

I have decided to keep my bald head and black tees and possibly even get a few more tattoos - but seek to regain the mind and mouth of the Psalmist who writes, **"Though you probe my heart and examine me at night, though you test me, you will find nothing; I have resolved that my mouth will not sin."** I'm not a thoughtless, wordless moron who has to moo like all of the other cows driven by the expectations of those I encounter on the road. I am an intelligent man of God who seeks to represent my Father well in all that I think, say and do. May God purify my heart, mind and mouth for His glory.

---

3 But among you there must not be even a hint of sexual immorality, or of any kind of impurity, or of greed, because these are improper for God's holy people. 4 Nor should there be obscenity, foolish talk or coarse joking, which are out of place, but rather thanksgiving. Ephesians 5:3-4

PSALM 18

ROAD GEAR

1 I love you, O Lord, my strength. 2 The Lord is my rock, my fortress and my deliverer; my God is my rock, in whom I take refuge. He is my shield and the horn of my salvation, my stronghold. 3 I call to the Lord, who is worthy of praise, and I am saved from my enemies.

30 As for God, his way is perfect; the word of the Lord is flawless. He is a shield for all who take refuge in him. 31 For who is God besides the Lord? And who is the Rock except our God? 32 It is God who arms me with strength and makes my way perfect. 33 He makes my feet like the feet of a deer; he enables me to stand on the heights. 34 He trains my hands for battle; my arms can bend a bow of bronze. 35 You give me your shield of victory, and your right hand sustains me; you stoop down to make me great. 36 You broaden the path beneath me, so that my ankles do not turn.

Bikers know the importance of dressing appropriately. Protection for the hands, the skin, the eyes, and (for some) the head are all a part of riding. Leather is truly more of a shield against the wind and asphalt than it is a fashion statement. Wrap around sunglasses protect our eyes from wind and bugs. Without these, we are left vulnerable, uncomfortable and more likely to be injured.

Training is important. Whether you learned to ride from a friend or from a certified safety course, it's important to know what you are doing BEFORE straddling a bike. Far too many have injured themselves or worse by writing out a check and then hitting the road.

So it was Sam's first day on his new bike. He had had his jacket for weeks; the helmet carefully picked out and painted to match his new wheels. Gloves and jeans were seen as riding essentials. Sam, however, had decided to hold off until the next paycheck to purchase his motorcycle boots. He already had a pair he felt were fairly protective and the expense could wait.

Sam set out across town on a beautiful day to meet a friend for lunch decked out in all of the gear he owned including his favorite cowboy boots. He was not aware, however, that his gear was destined to fail him. At a slow speed, up a steep driveway, he crossed a speed bump and put his feet out to steady himself. The slick bottomed cowboy boots slipped on the pavement and gave way. Losing its precarious balance, the bike leaned too far and sent Sam sprawling onto the roadside as it went down. Fortunately, a scratched mirror and bruised ego were the only damages. He learned that day, however, the importance of proper footgear if you want to be an effective road warrior.

Pete was enjoying a leisurely ride on a beautiful day. It was warm so he stopped and took off his jacket and gloves. The cool air felt good against his skin wearing just shirtsleeves. The traffic slowed abruptly as his attention was momentarily diverted. When he looked up he was too close to the car in front. In reaction, he locked up the rear brakes, lost control and went down hard. Painful road rash was the extent of his injuries. A leather jacket and gloves would have served him well.

In Psalm 18, the writer acknowledges that God is the only proper attire for our daily struggles and battles. He is our shield against the arrows the enemy fires at us. He is a stronghold we can run to and be protected. God arms us with strength we don't naturally possess making our way straight, our footsteps sure and our defense effective. If we are not clothed in God's righteousness, strength and character, we are ill prepared to handle the daily battles of anger, sexual temptation, depression and addictions, to mention just a few.

Notice though in verse 34 that this is not an ability instantaneously received for the asking. David speaks of God training him for the battle. The truth is that there are two kinds of protection mentioned here and we need them both. The first kind is the sort we run to and hide behind, meaning the fortress or the shield. This kind is instantaneous and offers shelter when we are under sudden attack, being hunted down or assaulted with a barrage of arrows.

The second kind of protection is the kind we have to learn over time. Depending on our willingness to grow and change, this can be a lengthy process. To learn to use weapons skillfully, a soldier must be committed to his training and his instructor. In the spiritual realm, God teaches us the skills we need and gives us the necessary tools to be effective in battle through times of reading the scripture and prayer. We will miss it if we depend upon ourselves and our own abilities. As in riding, the wrong training, techniques and gear can be disastrous.

So begin to develop a close relationship with God. Invest in something more than "chat prayers" and spend considerable time on your knees and searching the scriptures. You may even want to seek out an accountability partner; someone of the same gender, who seeks a mutual relationship of honest and regular dialogue and prayer. Such a partner helps to keep us consistent in our spiritual development. Then, allow the Lord to teach you what you need to know to prepare for the ride of your life.

———————————————

10 Finally, be strong in the Lord and in his mighty power. 11 Put on the full armor of God so that you can take your stand against the devil's schemes. 12 For our struggle is not against flesh and blood, but against the rulers, against the authorities, against the powers of this dark world and against the spiritual forces of evil in the heavenly realms. 13 Therefore put on the full armor of God, so that when the day of evil comes, you may be able to stand your ground, and after you have done everything, to stand. 14 Stand firm then, with the belt of truth buckled around your waist, with the breastplate of righteousness in place, 15 and with your feet fitted with the readiness that comes from the gospel of peace. 16 In addition to all this, take up the shield of faith, with which you can extinguish all the flaming arrows of the evil one. 17 Take the helmet of salvation and the sword of the Spirit, which is the word of God. 18 And pray in the Spirit on all occasions with all kinds of prayers and requests. With this in mind, be alert and always keep on praying for all the saints. Ephesians 6: 10-18

PSALM 19

RIDING BEHIND THE CLAMPETTS

7 The law of the Lord is perfect, reviving the soul. The statutes of the Lord are trustworthy, making wise the simple. 8 The precepts of the Lord are right, giving joy to the heart. The commands of the Lord are radiant, giving light to the eyes. 9 The fear of the Lord is pure, enduring forever. The ordinances of the Lord are sure and altogether righteous. 10 They are more precious than gold, than much pure gold; they are sweeter than honey, than honey from the comb. 11 By them is your servant warned; in keeping them there is great reward.

Jimmy and I were cruising down a two lane country road when we suddenly found ourselves in a scene from the Beverly Hillbillies. In front of us was an old pick-up truck moving at a snail's pace burdened by a load of home furnishings haphazardly stacked beyond the limits of common sense and safety. Fumes from the truck were toxic and visions of falling debris entered our minds. Much to our frustration, the yellow road sign read, "No Passing Next 10 Miles" underscored by two bright yellow lines on the asphalt below. It wasn't so much that we were in a hurry as we were concerned that gravity would soon prevail and we would find ourselves navigating through a cascading assortment of junk. No sooner had we thought it when our worst nightmare materialized as a mattress fell from the truck.....followed by a lamp, a barbeque and a bouncing storage tub. Jimmy went left while I went right; both escaping disaster by only a few inches.

I'm not sure if he was more scared or angry, but Jimmy continued his path to the left, ignoring the double yellow lines, as he passed "Uncle Jed and Cousin Jethro." He was freed from the truck only to encounter an oncoming vehicle, once again escaping disaster by inches. Nerves now shattered and adrenaline pumping at a dangerous rate, we both thought it best to just pull over and surrender the road to the Clampets.

So, what's the lesson here? While the truck disobeyed the laws of safety and common sense, Jimmy let frustration get the best of him and he disobeyed the laws of the state. Both contributed to a near fatal incident. Laws (human, natural and spiritual) are given for our safety and well being. Break these laws and you venture out on your own, taking your life into your own hands.

Psalm 19 has a plan and a road map for our journey that speaks of six kinds of laws that bring safety and prosperity to our lives. It's all based on knowing who God is and deciding to live life his way.

1. **The Law v7a** (The Ten Commandments) Imagine a world where there was no murder, no lying and no stealing. Imagine a world where people were content with what they had and did not lust for what was not theirs.

2. **The Statutes v7b** (Permanent Rules) An example of this would be God's universal law of sowing and reaping. We will never harvest good things out of our lives if we don't

plant quality seed now. We can count on this rule because it is one of God's permanent principles upon which he founded the universe.

3. **Precepts v8a** (Directions for Conduct)   When we follow God's direction for how we are to act and treat one another, he promises joy. The best guide for how we ought to treat one another is to ask ourselves, "How would we like to be treated?"

4. **Commands v8b** (Those written in the Bible as well as those spoken to us by God's Spirit each day.) God's commands (of which there are many more than just ten) are said to be "radiant….giving light to the eyes." So, even when we can't see how one of God's commandments could possibly be that important (i.e. "double yellow lines"), we must trust that he knows what he is doing.

5. **The Fear of the Lord v9a** (Reverential Awe) Regarding God with awe and respect is a lifelong pursuit and will continue into eternity, for the more we know about Him, the more we find there is to know. Worship, as a lifestyle, reminds us daily of who God is and who we are not; of what God can do and what we cannot.

6. **Ordinances v9b** (Things God has predestined and set into motion.) Everything God has said is pure gold; of great value and practical benefit for our journey. When we partake of what God says and let it become part of our lives, we find it is sweet….sweeter than honey. God promises reward to those who build their lives on what he has said.

24 Therefore everyone who hears these words of mine and puts them into practice is like a wise man who built his house on the rock. 25 The rain came down, the streams rose, and the winds blew and beat against that house; yet it did not fall, because it had its foundation on the rock. 26 But everyone who hears these words of mine and does not put them into practice is like a foolish man who built his house on sand. 27 The rain came down, the streams rose, and the winds blew and beat against that house, and it fell with a great crash.   Matthew 7:24-27

PSALM 20

BIKER COLORS

---

1 May the Lord answer you when you are in distress; may the name of the God of Jacob protect you. 2 May he send you help from the sanctuary and grant you support from Zion. 3 May he remember all your sacrifices and accept your burnt offerings. Selah 4 May he give you the desire of your heart and make all your plans succeed. 5 We will shout for joy when you are victorious and will lift up our banners in the name of our God. May the Lord grant all your requests. 6 Now I know that the Lord saves his anointed; he answers him from his holy heaven with the saving power of his right hand. 7 Some trust in chariots and some in horses, but we trust in the name of the Lord our God. 8 They are brought to their knees and fall, but we rise up and stand firm. 9 O Lord, save the king! Answer us when we call!

You can see them any place there is a sizeable gathering of bikers. Riders are patched and wearing their colors… proudly proclaiming the name under which they ride. This affords them brotherhood, safety and a sense of clout. Sometimes you even see these colors defended with strong words, muscle or even blood, counting on the strength of numbers to back them up.

It's not unlike the knights of the Middle Ages or soldiers of ancient biblical times who went to battle under a king's banner and colors. The protection offered by the banner was only as durable as the strength of the name under which they rode.   The name also offered brotherhood, safety and a sense of clout.

Whose patch are you wearing? Who's standing behind you? Perhaps you're a loner and choose to wear no one's name. So, where do you turn when you need help? Think about it before you answer because a truthful response says a lot about who you are and where you place your trust.   The Psalm writer here gives a list of those things he expects God to do for those who seek him out in times of trouble.   God is able to offer an answer to difficult questions, protection from enemies, help and support in times of trouble, grant specific requests for our needs and give success in our endeavors.

It is then pointed out how some trust in their chariots and some in their horses to get them through the tough situations . The chariot and the horse were considered the ultimate war machine in biblical times.   Nothing could outpace, outmaneuver or outlast this revolutionary means of fighting a war. They seemed a necessity for any king who wanted to gain the upper hand in a war or battle. But the writer declares, "...but we trust in the name of the Lord our God!"

So in your everyday struggles, what is the most important thing that gives you the advantage?   Is it your coolness, your toughness, your looks, your muscle, your job, money, the bike you ride or the patch on your back? Any of these things are shaky at best and are subject to the economy, to illness, age and any number of things we encounter in this life. The writer points out that those who mistakenly place their trust in the wrong places will be brought to their knees and will ultimately fall.

Compare this to those who trust in the name of the Lord as their source of help. Instead of falling, they rise up and stand firm! The name of the Lord is powerful! In fact, we are told that his is the name above every other name. When we live under his banner and accept his lordship over our lives, we can know his peace and presence in any situation. We are not in charge anymore and we are not subjected to the whims of life that threaten to undo us. He is in control and everything in our lives answers to him. And for you loners, you need not wear an actual patch, except for the one that you wear on your heart.

---

15 Out of his mouth comes a sharp sword with which to strike down the nations. "He will rule them with an iron scepter." He treads the winepress of the fury of the wrath of God Almighty. 16 On his robe and on his thigh he has this name written: KING OF KINGS AND LORD OF LORDS. Revelation 19:15-16

PSALM 21

THE GRAND PRIZE

4/9/13

1 "O Lord, the king rejoices in your strength. How great is his joy in the victories you give! 2 You have granted him the desire of his heart and have not withheld the request of his lips. 3 You welcomed him with rich blessings and placed a crown of pure gold on his head. 4 He asked you for life, and you gave it to him- length of days, for ever and ever. 5 Through the victories you gave, his glory is great; you have bestowed on him splendor and majesty. 6 Surely you have granted him eternal blessings and made him glad with the joy of your presence. 7 For the king trusts in the Lord; through the unfailing love of the Most High he will not be shaken.

It's Saturday morning, cool but sunny and clear, and you have a great day planned. Throwing on leathers, you meet your buddies at the local coffee hang out to stage for the ride. Arriving just a little early, you are greeted by slaps on the back, warm hugs and hand shakes all around with a cup of steaming hot brew...just the way you like it, thrust into your hand. You clearly belong...this is your crowd and it feels good to be a part of it.

You are soon off and headed down the road for the big fundraiser. Thousands of bikes, good music, prizes, crowds of people, your best friends and the staple of every biker's diet...the lowly hamburger, make for the perfect day. (Even a simple burger tastes great after a long ride.)

You and your buddies appropriately ooh and aah over the show bikes and take a tour through the vendors just to make sure there is nothing you can't live without.

They give away the first few raffle prizes....gift certificates, a few pieces of leather and you make sure you are present as you fish around in your pocket for the ticket. No luck... but not that you really care. More music, more fun and a few more prizes. You find yourself thinking that life is pretty good and couldn't get much better. Just for the sake of principle, you stick around for the grand prize drawing though you were ready to head for home an hour ago. Those words, "must be present to win" keep you lingering. After all, who in their right mind would pass up the chance to win a new Road King?

The moment arrives and everyone looks at their ticket for the fifth time that day. You think to yourself that you wish you had a dollar for every worthless stub you have taken home over the years. The number is announced and you look blankly at your ticket...then look a second and a third time. Maybe your eyes are playing tricks on you or...could it be that you have won the grand prize? WOW...you get your friend to double check for you then run forward to claim your new bike.

This is the scene that Psalm 21 is describing; the overwhelming favor of God. He gives victory in our lives over circumstances. We don't have to manipulate or scramble in our own strength to establish ourselves. God is clearly responsible and deserves the credit for the good things we enjoy. He welcomes us with rich blessings. It's like a young person coming home to his father from college or a long trip. He is received with open arms, hugs and kisses. Love and acceptance are ours whenever we enter the presence of our God. And if we have sinned, there is forgiveness and mercy for the repentant heart.

But these blessings are not just for this life. They are lasting...eternal when we trust in him. Knowing God is joyful, a lifelong adventure, satisfying and like winning the grand prize. Life just doesn't get any better. In him, our lives are secure and his love insures our stability.

———————————

3 We proclaim to you what we have seen and heard, so that you also may have fellowship with us. And our fellowship is with the Father and with his Son, Jesus Christ. 4 We write this to make your joy complete.   1John 1:3-4

PSALM 22 2/22/13

STRANDED AND ALONE

---

1 My God, my God, why have you forsaken me? Why are you so far from saving me, so far from the words of my groaning? 2 O my God, I cry out by day, but you do not answer, by night, and am not silent. 3 Yet you are enthroned as the Holy One; you are the praise of Israel. 4 In you our fathers put their trust; they trusted and you delivered them. 5 They cried to you and were saved; in you they trusted and were not disappointed. 6 But I am a worm and not a man, scorned by men and despised by the people. 7 All who see me mock me; they hurl insults, shaking their heads: 8 "He trusts in the Lord; let the Lord rescue him. Let him deliver him, since he delights in him." 9 Yet you brought me out of the womb; you made me trust in you even at my mother's breast. 10 From birth I was cast upon you; from my mother's womb you have been my God. 11 Do not be far from me, for trouble is near and there is no one to help.

14 I am poured out like water, and all my bones are out of joint. My heart has turned to wax; it has melted away within me. 15 My strength is dried up like a potsherd, and my tongue sticks to the roof of my mouth; you lay me in the dust of death. 16 Dogs have surrounded me; a band of evil men has encircled me, they have pierced my hands and my feet. 17 I can count all my bones; people stare and gloat over me. 18 They divide my garments among them and cast lots for my clothing. 19 But you, O Lord, be not far off; O my Strength, come quickly to help me. 20 Deliver my life from the sword, my precious life from the power of the dogs. 21 Rescue me from the mouth of the lions; save me from the horns of the wild oxen. 22 I will declare your name to my brothers; in the congregation I will praise you.

It was our first trip to the Laughlin River Run in Southern Nevada. The joke of the week was, "It's a hundred and thirty degrees in Laughlin...but it's a dry heat." While walking across the black top I couldn't figure out why I was stepping in so much gum. But it wasn't gum! It was the soles of my shoes melting onto the pavement beneath me.

Not knowing what to expect, that year I rode my bike while my wife and kids pulled an empty motorcycle trailer behind the truck. After a great week of the usual festivities, we loaded up and began our climb out of the river valley, back into the high desert and home. It wasn't long before we noticed a man standing next to his bike on the side of the road. It was the middle of the day and as the smoke rolled out from beneath his motor, I knew that this couldn't be good! The family and I pulled over to see if we could help and were greeted by the most grateful man we had ever met. As we handed him some water he began, "Man! I was #@$!!!% until you came along!" He continued, "It's a hundred plus degrees out here and I've blown a head gasket! I've got no water, no trailer and no tools. What a god-send you are!" To which I replied, "You have no idea!" (I said this because it is our desire to always be used by God to serve our fellow bikers.) So, we loaded his bike onto the trailer and took him about three hundred miles to his home. After refusing the wad of cash he tried to hand us, we left, pleased to know that we had helped.

Only a biker will appreciate this story; being broken down in the desert, on a bike, hundreds of miles from home.

Unlike a car that has some shade and perhaps supplies, when a bike breaks down, you are truly stranded and often alone. It's a horribly desperate and helpless feeling.

In Psalm 22 we see a man's desperation that far exceeds anything most of us have ever experienced. It describes crucifixion (nailing a criminal to a wooden cross) hundreds of years before it was practiced by the Roman Empire. And so our writer cries out (just as Jesus Christ would five hundred years later) "My God! Why have you forsaken me?" "I am surrounded [naked and humiliated]...I am poured out [beaten and weak], ...all my bones are out of joint [muscles and ligaments are torn from their rightful place], ...my heart is like wax; it has melted within me [chest cavity fills with fluid]. My strength is dried up...my tongue clings to my jaws [dehydration]; you have brought me to the dust of death." Hey! This guy is in REAL pain. He is thirsty, alone and believes that his god has abandoned him.

Suddenly, being stranded on the side of the highway doesn't seem like much, but the truth is, pain and loneliness are relative. When a splinter of wood is lodged beneath your fingernail, YOU'RE IN PAIN! At that moment, it doesn't matter how much worse another's misfortune might be - YOUR finger hurts! And so the lessons of Christ's pain and loneliness upon the cross (as seen in this Psalm) apply to us as well, no matter how great or small our predicament.

Christ who was abandoned by family, friends and his heavenly Father who could not look on the sin that was laid upon him (yours and mine) prayed nonetheless, "Be not far from me!" God is always there whether or not we can see, feel or hear him. He was in the jungles of Vietnam and the beaches of Normandy and he stands alongside a stranded biker just outside of Laughlin, Nevada. You and I in our turmoil may forget or doubt that God will never leave us, but Jesus did not.

Rescued or not, God remains God and, like Jesus, I will declare his greatness no matter what! The Psalmist closes his song with a grand finale of praise and adoration and declaration of the greatness of God! "I will declare your name to my brethren; In the midst of the assembly I will praise you!"

Feeling stranded and alone? Look to God who is willing and able to rescue you. Sooner or later, in his perfect timing, he will send someone along with a truck and a trailer and a bottle of cool water. And even if he doesn't - he is still there beside you.

_____

God has said, "Never will I leave you; never will I forsake you." So we say with confidence, "The Lord is my helper; I will not be afraid." Hebrews 13:5-6

PSALM 23 2/26/13

RUNNING WITH THE PACK

1 The Lord is my shepherd, I shall not be in want. 2 He makes me lie down in green pastures, he leads me beside quiet waters, 3 he restores my soul. He guides me in paths of righteousness for his name's sake. 4 Even though I walk through the valley of the shadow of death, I will fear no evil, for you are with me; your rod and your staff, they comfort me. 5 You prepare a table before me in the presence of my enemies. You anoint my head with oil; my cup overflows. 6 Surely goodness and love will follow me all the days of my life, and I will dwell in the house of the Lord forever.

Bikers like to think of themselves as independent, "the lone wolf" and in some cases just plain rebellious. Truth is, I have met very few who live alone and enjoy it. In fact, some people will do anything just to belong. Buy a bike, join a club and get a tattoo - whatever it takes! Then suddenly, those who once proclaimed uniqueness are now simply a part of the rolling leather clad masses - all of whom continue to proclaim their individuality. Remember the last rally you went to? What color leather was almost everyone wearing?

The trouble is, people end up compromising safety and ideals to join the crowd. The word "brother" can mean a lot to some. With it comes a sense of security and acceptance - but at what cost? The need for such belonging is, nevertheless, a part of what makes us human. We need connections on several different levels if we are to be fulfilled. Sooner or later, even the most independent of us needs relationships and community. King David (Psalm 23) understood that deep down, we are not lone wolves - we're sheep; a great big flock of sheep!

A young man I once knew accompanied me to a popular motorcycle rally. He came from a family that was not close and often hostile towards one another. He grew up, therefore, with little sense of belonging and acceptance. To fill the void he began to ride motorcycles and it was there that he saw his opportunity to belong. At first he rode with us, a few Christian brothers and friends but before long he began to follow and emulate a rougher crowd. They surrounded him and embraced him and called him "brother," but really they were just preparing to use him. (Funny? I have two brothers and we love each other very much - but I can't ever remember actually calling one of them "brother." Some things just don't need to be said.) He tried to look and act the part but to me he never did seem believable. He wasn't himself anymore; he was just a weak carbon copy of them.

Sadly, I watched him at this particular rally as he continued to drift away from us. I knew that the choices he was making and the group he was hanging with would soon lead him away - not just from us but also from the man he really was and wanted to be. Belonging to this crowd, however, was more important than his inner faith and ideals. Soon, we no longer recognized him. He was gone.

David may have agreed that we need to be a part of something bigger, but he also recognized the need for a leader, a shepherd who would keep us on the path and out of the bushes. So he declares that the Lord is his Shepherd...the Good Shepherd.

With God as our shepherd, we are led down paths of righteousness...making good decisions that do not lead to our destruction. We need never fear when we are his sheep for the Lord sees danger up ahead and will stick by us, defending us from those things that seek our demise. The rod and staff (his standards and laws) are not there to beat the sheep or strike us into submission but to protect us from our enemies and pull us back from the edge of the cliff when we get too close.

As if this is not enough, we are the objects of his favor and blessing. Rather than lead us into places where we will be forced to compromise and thus be put in danger, our shepherd leads us into places where his sheep will be followed by goodness and love all their days. When Jesus calls us "brother" he has no ulterior motive. He really loves us and cares for us.

Ever wonder why there are so many references in the Bible to people as sheep? Perhaps it is because we aren't very smart. (I understand that sheep can be pretty stupid!) It could be because we need constant care and protection like sheep. Leave them alone for just a moment and they wander into danger. It could also be because sheep never go it alone. They are always seen in a flock - a group. Not only do we need a good shepherd, we need each other. We need a family, a church, and a good flock with which to spend our time. We need to love and to be loved. We need to receive and we need to give. We need to be heard and we need to hear others. We really do need each other!

Solitude can be a good thing. I love riding alone with nothing but the wind in my face and the sound of my v-twin beneath me. But I need to ride to a place where I will meet up with those who love and care about me; who give me purpose and boundaries. If you ride alone all the time, you're missing it. There is a family somewhere waiting for you to come to the table and a Good Shepherd who wants to meet you.

Jesus said to His disciples, 34 "A new command I give you: Love one another. As I have loved you, so you must love one another. 35 By this all men will know that you are my disciples, if you love one another." John 13:34-35

PSALM 24

A SHARP DRESSED MAN

1 The earth is the Lord's, and everything in it, the world, and all who live in it; 2 for he founded it upon the seas and established it upon the waters. 3 Who may ascend the hill of the Lord? Who may stand in his holy place? 4 He who has clean hands and a pure heart, who does not lift up his soul to an idol or swear by what is false. 5 He will receive blessing from the Lord and vindication from God his Savior.

The story is told of a biker who was riding through the country one sunny Sunday morning when he realized that this was the Lord's Day and he remembered what he had learned from his mother as a small boy. As he pulled into the parking lot of a little church he immediately noticed the stares and the people whispering. His helmet had mashed his long hair and his jeans were covered by leather chaps which were in turn covered by dust. Once inside the church, the feeling of being welcome evaded him, but he took a seat anyway. After a few minutes had passed the pastor approached the biker and suggested, "Sir. Perhaps you should go home and pray and ask God how he would dress if he were to come to this church." Without an argument the biker simply got up and left. The following Sunday, however, he returned and his reception was about the same. After having taken a seat the pastor once again approached him and said, "Sir? Did I not ask you to pray

and seek God as to how he would dress if he were to come to this church?" "I did!" said the biker. "Well, what did he say?" asked the preacher. "He said that he had never been to this church and was unlikely to ever come in the near future."

What does it take to be able to come into God's presence? Do we need a shirt and tie? A suit? Do we need to "clean up our act" before coming to God or to church? Perhaps we should stop smoking first or sanitize our language. The Bible says that the one who is welcome to stand in the holy places is one who "has clean hands and a pure heart." Wow! That leaves every one of us outside sitting on the steps. And that is exactly why Jesus came and died on the cross on our behalf, as a sacrifice for our unclean hands and impure hearts. The Bible says, **"There is no one righteous, not even one."** (Romans 3:10) But it goes on to say that there IS a righteousness that **"comes through faith in Jesus Christ to all who believe."** (Roman 3:22) It also says, **"While we were still sinners, Christ died for us."** (Romans 5:8) As for "cleaning up our act" we are clearly told that **"It is by grace that you are saved; and not of yourselves: it is a GIFT of God."** (Ephesians 2:8)

The only way to have "clean hands and a pure heart" is to have them washed in the blood of Jesus. That is, to come before God and say, "Yep! I'm a sinner. I have no excuses. But I have confessed my sinfulness to you God and have accepted your son Jesus Christ as my Lord and Savior." Too bad that country preacher didn't understand this. All the showers and clean clothes in the world would not have ever made that biker ready for Sunday services. What made him ready was his repentant heart and a desire to come and worship. And when Jesus is in your heart, you're the best dressed man in town."

---

9 ...if you confess with your mouth, "Jesus is Lord," and believe in your heart that God raised him from the dead, you will be saved. 10 For it is with your heart that you believe and are justified, and it is with your mouth that you confess and are saved." Romans 10:9-10

PSALM 25 *4/0/13*

DING-A-LING

---

1 To you, O Lord, I lift up my soul; 2 in you I trust, O my God. Do not let me be put to shame, nor let my enemies triumph over me. 3 No one whose hope is in you will ever be put to shame, but they will be put to shame who are treacherous without excuse. 4 Show me your ways, O Lord, teach me your paths; 5 guide me in your truth and teach me, for you are God my Savior, and my hope is in you all day long. 6 Remember, O Lord, your great mercy and love, for they are from of old.

You see them everywhere. You may even own one. They're sold anywhere bikers are found. It's that little shiny trinket on the bottom of many a bike fondly referred to as a biker bell. Widely believed (tongue in cheek for some) to be infused with magical powers, the little brass relic or fetish is credited with the ability to chase away road demons thereby keeping both the bike and rider safe.

Maybe you don't believe in biker bells. Well then, let me ask you, "Where do you place your faith and trust?" Who looks out for you and insures your safety? Do you place your faith in all the leather you can stand to wear? Your own impeccable riding ability? Loud pipes? A DOT approved helmet? A flashy, showy, attention-grabbing bike? These things are all certainly safety measures but

86

they won't do you much good if someone on a cell phone happens to run a red light.

In truth, our hope for our safety needs to be in the right place...not focused on a little piece of brass, mass-produced by some company seeking to make a buck. The psalm writer reminds us that those who hope in the Lord have REAL security that lasts. For he does not ever forget us - EVER! Unlike the little bell that gets tarnished, covered with oil and road grime and soon loses its shiny newness, the Lord remains pure, faithful, unchanged and more beautiful the more we get to know him.

It is he who teaches us his ways and guides us in his truth. His mercy and love are timeless. They are always and forever extended towards us. The bell could lose its luster or fall off, but trusting in God is tangible and certain. Those who hope in him, we are told, are never put to shame.

Now, don't get us wrong. Motorcycles, like most anything else that is noisy and goes fast, can be dangerous. Good people, even Christians, die on motorcycles. But if you're looking for protection from road demons, begin with a faith in God Almighty, Creator of the universe before trusting in a manmade bell.

---

15 He [Jesus] is the image of the invisible God, the firstborn over all creation. 16 For by him all things were created: things in heaven and on earth, visible and invisible, whether thrones or powers or rulers or authorities; all things were created by him and for him. 17 He is before all things, and in him all things hold together. Colossians 1:15-17

PSALM 26 ₃|₈ ¹³

HOG TALES

---

1 Vindicate me, O Lord, for I have led a blameless life; I have trusted in the Lord without wavering. 2 Test me, O Lord, and try me, examine my heart and my mind; 3 for your love is ever before me, and I walk continually in your truth. 4 I do not sit with deceitful men, nor do I consort with hypocrites; 5 I abhor the assembly of evildoers and refuse to sit with the wicked. 6 I wash my hands in innocence, and go about your altar, O Lord, 7 proclaiming aloud your praise and telling of all your wonderful deeds. 8 I love the house where you live, O Lord, the place where your glory dwells. 9 Do not take away my soul along with sinners, my life with bloodthirsty men, 10 in whose hands are wicked schemes, whose right hands are full of bribes. 11 But I lead a blameless life; redeem me and be merciful to me. 12 My feet stand on level ground; in the great assembly I will praise the Lord.

Every word in the Bible is true. But that does not mean that every person speaking in the Bible is speaking the truth. What we have here is yet another human being who is trying to sell himself as blameless. Romans 3:10 says, **"There is no one righteous, not even one..."** It goes on in verse 23 to say, **"...all have sinned and fall short of the glory of God..."**

How many times have we justified our own behavior even when we knew we were in the wrong? "Honest officer! I wasn't going that fast...I did stop at the stop sign...No! I

89

haven't been drinking." Most of us at one time or another would have said anything to keep out of trouble or out of jail. It's a natural self-defense mechanism in the best of us.

Sometimes we just like to "remember BIG" adding a little color and spice to the story. For bikers it centers on how fast I rode, how far I went, how I faced danger and averted certain disaster. If it's not the paint job I am planning and what it will cost, then it's the deal I am working, who I know and what they want to do for me. Why can't we just tell the truth? "It was a nice ride, not too far and a little windy."

David didn't need to present any other case to God than, **"...redeem me and be merciful to me."** I am a sinner. You are a sinner. We are all sinners! You may have never killed anyone, but have you ever wished someone dead? You may have never stolen anything (or gotten caught) but do you ever lay awake wanting something so very badly - that isn't yours to have? Jesus said that hatred was the same as murder and that to covet that which is not yours, is indeed a sin. In fact, a sin is not necessarily doing anything, but can be the omission of doing the right thing. So you see, one man may steal and another may lie. One struggles with lust while another is haunted by the demons of alcohol. One talks too much (i.e. gossip) while another harbors bitterness and unforgiveness in their heart. Sin is sin! It's all bad! It's all lethal to the human spirit. Just because I don't share your temptation doesn't mean that I am not tempted in another way. I stumble and am in need of God's grace and forgiveness.

David was indeed a godly man - even described as **"a man after God's own heart."** He wrote many beautiful songs to God and dedicated his life to God's service. Let's not forget, however, that David was guilty of lying, adultery and murder (see 2 Samuel chapters 11-12). So, while he was not like the **"deceitful...hypocrites"** or a member of the **"assembly of evildoers",** he did have his own sins and failures. We all do!

Where have you sinned? Where have you fallen short of what God would have wanted for you? Don't defend yourself. There is no need. After all, what have you done that God doesn't already know about? Yes, our God is a righteous God who punishes evil, but he is also gracious and merciful to those who humble themselves before him. Repeat after me, **"...redeem me and be merciful to me."** That's it! And trust him as your Lord and Savior.

If we confess our sins, he is faithful and just and will forgive us our sins and purify us from all unrighteousness. **1John 1:9**

PSALM 27

WHY WOULD YOU DROP A HARLEY?

1 The Lord is my light and my salvation-whom shall I fear? The Lord is the stronghold of my life-of whom shall I be afraid? 2 When evil men advance against me to devour my flesh, when my enemies and my foes attack me, they will stumble and fall. 3 Though an army besiege me, my heart will not fear; though war break out against me, even then will I be confident.

Years ago when I was first looking to buy a motorcycle my friend Gary and I went shopping. As we entered the first Harley shop we saw the beautiful bikes lined up in the window, each one reflecting the sunlight with a different color. We were both awestruck as I climbed aboard the biggest bike I could find. Soon a salesman casually approached us, watching as my thirty-inch legs stretched to reach the ground. I said, "Wow! Big bike! What happens if you drop one of these things?" Without any hesitation he looked at me and said, "You don't drop a Harley!"

The following weekend Gary and I continued our tour of dealerships in search of the perfect scooter. As we entered the store, this time it was Gary who first straddled a bike and just as before, a salesman appeared. Gary asked, "These things are pretty heavy. What happens if you drop one?" Now, keep in mind that this is a week later and we are at least seventy miles from the previous dealership when the salesman declares, "Oh - you don't drop a Harley," just as if everyone else knew that this was so.

It was week three as Gary and I entered into yet another Harley dealership. We had surmised by this time that there was certainly a conspiracy to convince new riders that it was impossible to actually drop a Harley-Davidson. Just as I jumped on a beautiful new Fat Boy, an eager salesman arrived. Smiling at Gary I asked, "Gee! These are pretty heavy motorcycles! What happens if you drop one?" (Gary mouthed in silence, "You don't drop a Harley!") A wounded look then came across the salesman's face as he replied, "Why would you want to drop a Harley?" I gave up - bought the bike and on my second day, contrary to the salesman's encouraging pitch, dropped my new Harley-Davidson! But THAT is another story.

These veteran riders and salesmen simply did not have it in their vocabulary to discuss the possibility of laying down one of these beautiful machines. While I am sure that they knew it happened from time to time, discussing the possibility was apparently some kind of unwritten taboo. It just wasn't in their thinking.

So many people today doubt God. They quickly attribute war, famine and natural disasters to God's lack of concern or involvement. For David, the writer of Psalm 27, such a thought was unthinkable. God was not only full of love, but also present for him in times of extreme stress. His life was tough. At times he was on the run. Night and day he roamed the wilderness seeking shelter and a safe place to hide. He slept in dark and unexplored caves. He suffered from cold, heat, rain, snow and wind.

But for David, it was unthinkable that God would desert him and ignore his calamity. It is not in God's character to forget his people or be apathetic about their pain. Some believe, "You don't drop a Harley!" But the Psalmist believed, "**The Lord is the stronghold of my life-of whom shall I be afraid?**" God was his light and salvation. When whole armies sought his life in the desert, he chose to be confident in the Lord's protection.

Like David, we must recognize that there is a profound difference between fact and truth. Facts are those things we come up against such as fear, conflict and evil. Truth, however, is where we need to focus and truth can only be found in God's word which reminds us that God does indeed love and care for his people. Our silly story illustrates a concept that was unthinkable to three motorcycle salesmen. David's confidence in his heavenly father illustrates how unthinkable it should be for us to doubt God and the promises of his written Word.

─────────────────────────────

Keep your lives free from the love of money and be content with what you have, because God has said, "Never will I leave you…" Hebrews 13:5

PSALM 28

TRUE FRIENDS

---

3 Do not drag me away with the wicked, with those who do evil, who speak cordially with their neighbors but harbor malice in their hearts.

6 Praise be to the Lord, for he has heard my cry for mercy. 7 The Lord is my strength and my shield; my heart trusts in him, and I am helped. My heart leaps for joy and I will give thanks to him in song. 8 The Lord is the strength of his people, a fortress of salvation for his anointed one. 9 Save your people and bless your inheritance; be their shepherd and carry them forever.

You have probably heard someone say, "I wouldn't trade a single one of my biker friends for ten other people." Such is the conviction, loyalty and camaraderie commonly expressed throughout biker culture. We ride together, eat together, support each other, trade stories, weather crises together and just hang out. We give blood, raise funds for sick kids, do toy runs and proclaim emphatically our loyalty and love for each other.

Just like the psalmist, we would never want to be mentioned in the same breath with those we consider two faced or hypocritical. We are slow to believe that any of those with whom we ride would betray us by speaking cordially and positively with us but maligning our character as soon as we are out of earshot.

But the truth is that people everywhere are pretty much the same. Bikers, cowboys, suits and ties - it doesn't matter. There are many fine, outstanding people who ride motorcycles...and there are some we need to watch out for. Just like at school, in business or at church, people are people and no group can claim a monopoly on all or even most of the "good ones." Just as no group can be labeled completely bad. When it comes down to it, we pretty much pick our friends within a narrow comfort zone determined by us. We define good ones and bad ones based on those with whom we feel most at home.

In this passage, the writer rejoices in the Lord and in the joy of knowing him. Let me ask you a question: If you were to name the ten friends you can most rely on when the chips are down, would God be among them? Would you even think of him in such a context?

David seems to recognize the worth of knowing the Lord. He essentially is saying, "Lord, you are my God and I would not trade your favor for any number of other people, who in their humanness, could let me down." Instead, he chooses to trust God and focus his attention on God's truth. Can we say the same? Is God among our best friends?

Even our truest buddies are subject to human weakness and error and will let us down from time to time. But God is truly and forever worth our trust, our obedience and heartfelt thanks for all that he has done for us. He does indeed hear our cry for mercy. He is strength, a shield and a fortress in time of trouble. When we place our confidence and trust in him, we are helped.

Jesus said, "I no longer call you servants, because a servant does not know his master's business. Instead, I have called you friends, for everything that I learned from my Father I have made known to you." John 15:15

PSALM 29

POWER TO SPARE

---

1 Ascribe to the Lord, O mighty ones, ascribe to the Lord glory and strength. 2 Ascribe to the Lord the glory due his name; worship the Lord in the splendor of his holiness. 3 The voice of the Lord is over the waters; the God of glory thunders, the Lord thunders over the mighty waters. 4 The voice of the Lord is powerful; the voice of the Lord is majestic. 5 The voice of the Lord breaks the cedars; the Lord breaks in pieces the cedars of Lebanon. 6 He makes Lebanon skip like a calf, Sirion like a young wild ox. 7 The voice of the Lord strikes with flashes of lightning. 8 The voice of the Lord shakes the desert; the Lord shakes the Desert of Kadesh. 9 The voice of the Lord twists the oaks and strips the forests bare. And in his temple all cry, "Glory!" 10 The Lord sits enthroned over the flood; the Lord is enthroned as King forever. 11 The Lord gives strength to his people; the Lord blesses his people with peace.

Power! It's a common theme among hot rod and motorcycle enthusiasts. All it takes is the growl of a motor and smoke from a rear tire to awaken a crowd of men. They explode to their feet with a cheer at the combination of paint, chrome and horsepower. We often hear of motorcycle rallies with names like "Thunder on the Mountain" and "Rumble in the Desert." Don't get me wrong, there's nothing like the feeling one gets from a powerful v-twin motor between their knees, but hey, it's just a motorcycle - right?

Nature (God's handiwork) is far more powerful and awesome than any man made machine. The winds of a tornado can snap a tree like a toothpick and the waves of a tsunami can devastate a coastline in seconds. We use words like "awesome" and "powerful" far too quickly, forgetting that God in all of his glory is the only one truly worthy of such adjectives. Can any paint job on a custom bike compare with a tropical sunset? Can the glimmer of new chrome compare to the glimmer of sunshine on freshly fallen snow? Hey! I really like my bike - but I worship God.

God has no need to even lift a finger to manage the affairs of Earth. He has only to speak and the gigantic cedars break, nations are set in motion, lightning flashes, deserts shake and whole forests are stripped bare. It kind of reminds me of the pictures we saw when Mount Saint Helens blew her top. But unlike a volcano that erupts once and then sits silent for years, God's power is established forever and no one can change that.

We glorify athletes, movie stars and rock legends as if they have created with their own hands the planets and the moon and the stars. It is God and God alone who deserves words like "glory and strength and splendor." Who else can we say is truly worthy to sit on a celestial throne?

His strength is not the kind which flexes its muscle one day and is gone the next. Our God's power is steady and unwavering. He shares that power with us; power to live, strength to overcome and confidence to believe in a God that we cannot see. Man inspired power is fleeting and repeatedly threatens to disappear or ruin its possessor.

Machines blow and chrome rusts and testosterone diminishes with time - but GOD is GOD forever.

---

3 For though we live in the world, we do not wage war as the world does. 4 The weapons we fight with are not the weapons of the world. On the contrary, they have divine power to demolish strongholds. 2Corinthian 10:3-4

PSALM 30 ᴴ⁄₆/₁³

BIKER DOWN

1 I will exalt you, O Lord, for you lifted me out of the depths and did not let my enemies gloat over me. 2 O Lord my God, I called to you for help and you healed me. 3 O Lord, you brought me up from the grave; you spared me from going down into the pit. 4 Sing to the Lord, you saints of his; praise his holy name. 5 For his anger lasts only a moment, but his favor lasts a lifetime; weeping may remain for a night, but rejoicing comes in the morning. 6 When I felt secure, I said, "I will never be shaken." 7 O Lord, when you favored me, you made my mountain stand firm; but when you hid your face, I was dismayed. 8 To you, O Lord, I called; to the Lord I cried for mercy: 9 "What gain is there in my destruction, in my going down into the pit? Will the dust praise you? Will it proclaim your faithfulness? 10 Hear, O Lord, and be merciful to me; O Lord, be my help." 11 You turned my wailing into dancing; you removed my sackcloth and clothed me with joy, 12 that my heart may sing to you and not be silent. O Lord my God, I will give you thanks forever.

Craig lay in a hospital bed...face flushed and body wracked with pain, moving as little as possible and periodically pushing the button that delivered his pain killer. A group of us stood around him encouraging, consoling and praying. More than anything we were just glad he had survived the accident that nearly took his life. Once again, an unthinking driver had turned left in front of a motorcycle that they did not see.

Due to a long recuperation, it was doubtful our friend Craig would still be employed. Rehab would be required to teach him new coping skills necessary for adapting to unfamiliar disabilities. Depression and hopelessness were ever present enemies to be fought.

But in spite of all this, Craig seemed strangely upbeat. He was barely two weeks into a long recovery yet confessed, "I see things differently now. My thinking seems to be changing since the accident. I know I've made some bad choices in the last year or two but in these past two weeks, I've grown what seems like 20 years. I'm reevaluating how I've treated myself and others."

No doubt about it, by his own admission, Craig had been in an elevator that was going down. The depths seemed to be opening up fast to swallow him whole. But like David, he was now recognizing the extent that God was willing to go to get his attention and lift him from the pit into which he had sunk. Rather than be angry with God and cast blame and become bitter, the psalm writer confesses that grieving and weeping were a process to go through much like a tunnel. Tunnels are a transition through an obstacle that bring us to the other side. The only thing dangerous about a tunnel is getting stuck in the middle. But if we are willing to press on, rejoicing and light will be there in the morning. Craig was beginning to accept this truth.

God can turn our **"wailing into dancing"** and our troubles into joy. Once we realize that our bad choices are leading to nothing good, we can give thanks even in our pain and begin to reevaluate our lives. There is a big difference between giving thanks to God **for** everything versus giving thanks **in** every situation thereby giving God an opportunity to illustrate his love, mercy and wisdom.

Countless bikers who have suffered accidents or personal setbacks have confessed the same thing. God is not to blame for our suffering but to be exalted because he uses adverse situations to bring us out of the depths of our own self-destruction. Don't get me wrong - most of these people were not initially happy for the adversity in their lives but after all was said and done, they confess that they would not trade it for the traps into which they were about to fall. God is faithful and helps us when we cry out to him.

_____

16 Be joyful always; 17 pray continually; 18 give thanks in all circumstances, for this is God's will for you in Christ Jesus. I Thessalonians 5:16-18

PSALM 31

4/12/13

SCOOTER TRASH

---

1 In you, O LORD, I have taken refuge; let me never be put to shame; deliver me in your righteousness. 2 Turn your ear to me, come quickly to my rescue; be my rock of refuge, a strong fortress to save me. 3 Since you are my rock and my fortress, for the sake of your name lead and guide me.

11 Because of all my enemies, I am the utter contempt of my neighbors; I am a dread to my friends— those who see me on the street flee from me. 12 I am forgotten by them as though I were dead; I have become like broken pottery. 13 For I hear the slander of many; there is terror on every side; they conspire against me and plot to take my life. 14 But I trust in you, O LORD; I say, "You are my God."

Before I was a biker, I was a pastor. As a general rule, pastors are loved and respected by their congregations and communities. We marry young couples, dedicate babies, are asked to pray before town meetings and are there when a family grieves the passing of someone close. Never did a Sunday go by but that one or more of the children at my church would run up to me and throw their arms around me and say, "Good morning Pastor. I love you!" It is good to know that you are loved and respected.

Years later I became a pastor to bikers. As you might expect, my looks changed. My head is shaved and I have

a beard. My ears are pierced and I have a couple of nice tattoos. I gave my suits and ties to the Salvation Army and bought some blue jeans and acquired a closet full of black tee shirts. I wear the mandatory flesh protecting leathers and dark wrap around sunglasses - but children no longer run up to me and tell me that they love me. I was in a grocery store the other day and noticed a mother pull her small child close to her as I walked by. I guess I was being profiled as "scooter trash."

I am the same man that I was when I pastored a local church. I still love people and want to help them any way that I can - only now I mostly pastor bikers. Perhaps for the first time, and only in a very small way, I can empathize with Viet Nam vets who went away innocent young men willing to serve their country, only to return to an ungrateful and hostile nation that saw them as villains and called them "baby killers." No wonder so many are still living that pain. Just last week a vet asked me, "Why did I survive? Why me? What makes me the fortunate one?"

Once again, for the record, we are sinners. We are ALL sinners! We have all lied, cheated, hated and killed if only with our eyes. As the Bible says, **"There is no one righteous; not even one."** All bikers are sinners - all vets are sinners - all pastors are sinners. And that is why we all need a savior. And so the Psalmist writes, "**In you, O LORD, I have taken refuge; let me never be put to shame; deliver me in YOUR righteousness.** " Suits or leathers, it makes no difference; our righteousness is found only in our relationship with Jesus Christ. Like a homeless person who comes into great wealth simply by being adopted into the Rockefeller family, our wealth of righteousness is found only in Jesus.

There will always be people who will see it as their duty to remind others that they are not good enough or not wearing the right clothes. For the Christian, we return to our **"rock of refuge, a strong fortress."** He is there to remind us daily that we are not trash, we are not villains and we are not unforgiven for our sin. And as he is there for us, we remember that we are there for him as well; as a witness of his abundant grace and mercy and as an ambassador of his love and kindness.

One day, all of those who know Jesus Christ as Lord and Savior, and who proclaim, **"You are my God,"** will come into his presence. There will no doubt be suits and ties, jeans and tee-shirts, bikers and businessmen, cowboys and surfers in heaven. We will all be the same in God's sight because of our righteousness in Jesus. None of us have sinned too much or traveled too far to escape his love and mercy. And those who trust in him will look on his face and he will say once and for all, **"Welcome home!"**

---

8 For it is by grace you have been saved, through faith—and this not from yourselves, it is the gift of God— 9 not by works, so that no one can boast. Ephesians 2:8-9

PSALM 32 7/14/13

RIDING FREE - TRULY FREE

1 Blessed is he whose transgressions are forgiven, whose sins are covered. 2 Blessed is the man whose sin the Lord does not count against him and in whose spirit is no deceit. 3 When I kept silent, my bones wasted away through my groaning all day long. 4 For day and night your hand was heavy upon me; my strength was sapped as in the heat of summer. Selah 5 Then I acknowledged my sin to you and did not cover up my iniquity. I said, "I will confess my transgressions to the Lord" - and you forgave the guilt of my sin. Selah

Ask any biker, read any testimony, even those which have been tattooed on flesh. Freedom remains a prominent theme for all who ride. There's something about being in the wind and the sun with the soothing rumble of a big V-twin beneath you that makes so many things right.

When I worked in an office, there would be days when the demands were greater than I could meet. I felt like a trapped animal cornered by the ringing of telephones and the screams of every deadline. Unlike any other stress reliever, twenty minutes in the wind could set me free even if for only a few moments. Though I had to once again face the chaos, a small grin would remain on my face as a result of my therapeutic ride.

There is another demand upon every life that many do not recognize or choose to acknowledge. Haunting memories and nagging guilt can be likened unto every phone that rings or deadline that demands. Every adulterous look, every half-truth and every thought of evil remains with us, demanding justice. We are, simply put, every one a sinner. We were born to sin. The cover of Christianity Today (a popular Christian publication) once displayed the photograph of a baby lying on the proverbial bearskin rug. Unlike any infant you have ever seen, however, this child bore (through the miracle of enhanced graphic arts) a tattoo on his right arm. It simply read "natural born sinner."

Christianity Today was making the point that sin is a seed and from it grows many sins and every sin committed binds us like chains until justice has been paid or freedom has been purchased. Psalm 32 is a voice celebrating such freedom. The Bible tells us that Jesus Christ died as a sacrifice for our sins - to set us free from the debt that we have incurred by being sinners. When we accept Christ and His gift of freedom, there is such a joy that - well, "If I have to explain, you wouldn't understand."

To keep silent about my sin is like being nauseated but refusing to throw up! Sin, like a bad burrito, will churn and eat at you from the inside out. Just let it go! Admit it -"I am a sinner!" It comes as a surprise to no one! I know I am a sinner. God knows that I am a sinner and everyone who knows me at all knows that I am a sinner. Freedom comes when I admit it and agree with what God says about me. That is what Jesus meant when He said, **"The truth shall**

set you free." Then all that remains is for us to accept God's gift of forgiveness offered us through Jesus.

Am I a sinner? Yes! Nevertheless, my debt has been paid and because of the love that has been given to me, I choose to give my very best to seeing that sin becomes the exception rather than the rule in my life. And I have a small grin on my face that says, **"Blessed** (or happy) **is he whose transgressions are forgiven, whose sins are covered."** What a feeling!

Riding free - truly free has little to do with what you ride or whether or not you wear a DOT approved helmet. Freedom comes from knowing that you have been forgiven and that your debt has been paid. I am free because Christ has set me free. The wind is so much sweeter and the ride so much more satisfying because someone far greater than I has made it so.

It is for freedom that Christ has set us free. Stand firm, then, and do not let yourselves be burdened again by a yoke of slavery. Galatians 5:1

PSALM 33

RESPECT

6 By the word of the Lord were the heavens made, their starry host by the breath of his mouth. 7 He gathers the waters of the sea into jars; he puts the deep into storehouses. 8 Let all the earth fear the Lord; let all the people of the world revere him. 9 For he spoke, and it came to be; he commanded, and it stood firm. 10 The Lord foils the plans of the nations; he thwarts the purposes of the peoples. 11 But the plans of the Lord stand firm forever, the purposes of his heart through all generations. 12 Blessed is the nation whose God is the Lord, the people he chose for his inheritance. 13 From heaven the Lord looks down and sees all mankind; 14 from his dwelling place he watches all who live on earth--15 he who forms the hearts of all, who considers everything they do. 16 No king is saved by the size of his army; no warrior escapes by his great strength. 17 A horse is a vain hope for deliverance; despite all its great strength it cannot save. 18 But the eyes of the Lord are on those who fear him, on those whose hope is in his unfailing love…"

My neighbor rides a "crotch-rocket" and I ride a Harley-Davidson. For years we have enjoyed the friendly banter that goes back and forth across the street regarding the virtues of American verses metric motorcycles. I was watching him from my porch one day as he was showing his bike to a friend. Their discussion was escalating from a casual show and tell to a plea for, "C'mon, let me ride it!"

My neighbor seemed reluctant to let his friend get on the bike but soon gave in to his begging.

The novice rider had barely thrown his leg over the seat when he started the motor. With the slightest twist of the throttle he was suddenly air born, a victim of throttle lock (a condition where the quick acceleration of a motorcycle does not allow for one to release the hand throttle). Like a missile he crossed our street, plowed my front lawn and buried the nose of the bike into a neighbor's garage door. There he sat stunned and embarrassed by his inability to control the beast, lucky to escape with a bruised ego and a lacerated desire to ride motorcycles.

I can remember the day I picked up my first Harley-Davidson. As the salesman was finishing up the paperwork, an old biker casually walked up to me. With his long hair and beard cascading down his face he looked at me with kind but very serious eyes and said, "As long as you respect her son, you'll be fine. Just don't ever disrespect her." It took me a few years to fully understand what he meant until I had seen enough stunt dummies injure themselves doing wheelies and burnouts. My neighbor's buddy had no respect for that street bike. It was lean and fast and no bike for a beginner, yet he ignored all of that and jumped into the saddle ill prepared. Would he have done the same with a rodeo bull? Would he have run through a thunderstorm waving an aluminum rod? Would he have dared swim with the sharks? Common sense says that we should respect those things that are awesome in power or in this case, speed.

"Give respect where respect is due" is what the Psalmist is saying. He describes God as the maker of the heavens and master of the oceans. All God had to do was SPEAK… and it was so! It stands to reason, then, that peoples and nations are not a threat to God. God is the One who is in control and so, **"Blessed is the nation whose God is the Lord."** All of us macho desperado types are warned that no one, not even kings, are saved by their armies and no warrior is saved by his strength. I've heard so many foolish men say things like, "When I see God I'm gonnna…!" Yeah! Sure you are! Truth is, when you see God, you're going to fall on your face and whimper like a puppy!

But it is not that God wants to frighten or inflict pain. (That street bike wasn't designed to throw people through garage doors.) No, in fact, "**the eyes of the Lord are on those who fear him. On those whose hope is in his unfailing love."** He desires friendship and fellowship with us as long as we understand who is God and who is mere man. We are so brave when our friends come around. We talk so big once we've had a few beers. But God is an awesome and mighty God who is not to be mocked or disrespected. He will not continue to put up with the foolishness of men forever. The Bible tells us that one day every knee will bow and every tongue will confess that Jesus Christ is Lord. Just imagine all of the presidents, all of the dictators, all of the mighty men of Wall Street, all of the tough guys and bullies kneeling before Jesus Christ and declaring that he is Lord! All of their power and influence and money will not help them then, not nearly as much as a healthy dose of respect would have helped them from the beginning.

28 Therefore, since we are receiving a kingdom that cannot be shaken, let us be thankful, and so worship God acceptably with reverence and awe, 29 for our "God is a consuming fire." Hebrews 12:28-29

PSALM 34

LIFE IS LIKE A ROAD

1 I will extol the Lord at all times; his praise will always be on my lips. 2 My soul will boast in the Lord; let the afflicted hear and rejoice. 3 Glorify the Lord with me; let us exalt his name together. 4 I sought the Lord, and he answered me; he delivered me from all my fears. 5 Those who look to him are radiant; their faces are never covered with shame. 6 This poor man called, and the Lord heard him; he saved him out of all his troubles. 7 The angel of the Lord encamps around those who fear him, and he delivers them. 8 Taste and see that the Lord is good; blessed is the man who takes refuge in him. 9 Fear the Lord, you his saints, for those who fear him lack nothing. 10 The lions may grow weak and hungry, but those who seek the Lord lack no good thing. 11 Come, my children, listen to me; I will teach you the fear of the Lord. 12 Whoever of you loves life and desires to see many good days, 13 keep your tongue from evil and your lips from speaking lies. 14 Turn from evil and do good; seek peace and pursue it. 15 The eyes of the Lord are on the righteous and his ears are attentive to their cry; 16 the face of the Lord is against those who do evil, to cut off the memory of them from the earth. 17 The righteous cry out, and the Lord hears them; he delivers them from all their troubles. 18 The Lord is close to the brokenhearted and saves those who are crushed in spirit. 19 A righteous man may have many troubles, but the Lord delivers him from them all…

Life has often been compared to a road. It is never perfect, sometimes good, paved in places and sometimes just dirt.

Modern day bandits for the motorcycle rider include sand, ice, gravel, debris, potholes or water in places unexpected and unwanted. Sometimes the pavement is newly surfaced and smooth and sometimes it can appear to be a road that civilization forgot decades ago. Sometimes roads are wide, sometimes narrow and occasionally cluttered by construction crews. And even when a road seems to be perfect in every way possible, there is always the chance for unexpected debris.

We were on our way back from Sturgis, South Dakota and working our way past miles and miles of Nebraska cornfields. Without drama or fanfare, the rear of the bike seemed to be sinking. After pulling our fully loaded cruiser to the side of the road and inspecting the tire I discovered what appeared to be a small metallic fragment. With the care of an experienced surgeon armed with rusty pliers I proceeded to remove a pair of road beaten finger nail clippers from my rear tire, leaving a hole big enough to insert one's index finger.

A day or two earlier, perhaps a week, a thoughtless driver had tossed a pair of clippers onto the road which brought our 1340cc's to a rolling stop. What makes the situation interesting is that fingernail clippers, not daggerish in design, had to be lying in the road in just such a manner so as to pose a threat to a tire. Fifty miles from anywhere we found those clippers in just the right position that brought our day to an unexpected halt.

This Psalm is full of promises we can hang onto. It includes promises for provision, support, protection, deliverance and blessing. However, we may be tempted to take in all of the wonderful promises and miss the greater truth altogether. Let us be clear, one CAN believe God's word! He says what he means when he declares he will deliver us from fear, remove shame for past deeds, hear us when we call out, and be a refuge and a source of supply for the needs of our lives. Too often however, we over simplify the scriptures, choosing to accept the wonderful promises but ignoring verses such as 19 which remind us that, **"A righteous man may have many troubles..."** We are surprised and caught off guard by adversity, wondering what we did to deserve such problems. The truth is, life just happens! It is full of ups and downs, potholes and weather and sometimes an occasional accident. The key to survival is knowing where to turn when trouble happens.

As we sat on the side of the road pondering our options I had completely dismissed using the cell phone since it had not worked in days. ("Can you hear me now?") After praying, the wife suggested that I give it one more try. With the understandable disgust of a man who was hot and tired and the proud owner of a newly flattened tire in the great state of Nebraska, I reluctantly flipped open my phone. Much to my surprise, IT WORKED!

We were rescued and on our way within hours bearing a new appreciation for roadside assistance and God's watch care over us. (Why had the phone not worked for days, but worked there and then on the side of the road? It is also interesting to note that it did not work again for another twenty-four hours.) Were we spared the hassle, the heat, the wait and the worry? No! But we were reminded again that even though, **"A righteous man may have many troubles…the Lord delivers him from them all."**

Remember that deliverance may not always look like we expect or would want. Sometimes we are indeed rescued from the hazards of the road and sometimes our deliverance comes as we grow and mature through tough times with God guiding and encouraging us along the way. Either way, you are never alone and never lost when you ride with God.

Jesus quoted the Old Testament prophet Isaiah saying, 4 "Prepare the way for the Lord, make straight paths for him. 5 Every valley shall be filled in, every mountain and hill made low. The crooked roads shall become straight, the rough ways smooth. " Luke 3:4-5

PSALM 35

Surviving the Fall

1 Contend, O Lord, with those who contend with me; fight against those who fight against me. 2 Take up shield and buckler; arise and come to my aid. 3 Brandish spear and javelin against those who pursue me. Say to my soul, "I am your salvation."

9 Then my soul will rejoice in the Lord and delight in his salvation. 10 My whole being will exclaim, "Who is like you, O Lord? You rescue the poor from those too strong for them, the poor and needy from those who rob them." 11 Ruthless witnesses come forward; they question me on things I know nothing about. 12 They repay me evil for good and leave my soul forlorn. 13 Yet when they were ill, I put on sackcloth and humbled myself with fasting. When my prayers returned to me unanswered, 14 I went about mourning as though for my friend or brother. I bowed my head in grief as though weeping for my mother. 15 But when I stumbled, they gathered in glee; attackers gathered against me when I was unaware. They slandered me without ceasing

23 Awake, and rise to my defense! Contend for me, my God and Lord. 24 Vindicate me in your righteousness, O Lord my God; do not let them gloat over me. 25 Do not let them think, "Aha, just what we wanted!" or say, "We have swallowed him up." 26 May all who gloat over my distress be put to shame and confusion; may all who exalt themselves over me be clothed with shame and disgrace. 27 May those who delight in my vindication shout for joy and gladness;

may they always say, "The Lord be exalted, who delights in the well-being of his servant." 28 My tongue will speak of your righteousness and of your praises all day long.

People can be really mean! Mean people are the best illustration of what a world without God looks like. They are the fall of man manifested in human form, illustrated by hate, violence, curses, lies, cheating, law suits and so much more. How many times have you wanted to take matters into your own hands? Do you sometimes lie awake at night and think about ways that you could get even or come up with a zinger of a comeback? Are you secretly happy when someone who has wronged you trips or is embarrassed, demoted or even injured? We have all been there at one time or another. It's human and it feels good - but it is not God's best.

I am a member of a Christian motorcycle ministry who wears a multi-colored patch on my vest which represents our organization. You may or may not know that in the motorcycle world such a patch, sometimes referred to as "colors" must be approved by the area's ruling motorcycle club or confederation of clubs. Because we are a motorcycle "ministry" and technically not a "club", most groups dismiss us and couldn't care less what patch we wear. Others, however, have gone to great extremes, even threatening violence, unless we complied with certain guidelines. It's just the biker way and the rules of the road.

Early on I would try to reason with the opponents of our patch, but my words usually fell on deaf ears. It was proposed to be a matter of protocol and respect for those who came before us or it could have just been an issue of control. I would lie awake at night and pray for their demise and for God to vindicate us. While I am sure that they were sleeping just fine, I tossed and turned at the injustice and was well on my way to developing an ulcer. It was then that I, in essence said, **"Contend, O Lord with those who contend with me; fight against those who fight against me."** But I didn't want God to work it out. No, I wanted him to consume the lot of them with fire! It wasn't until years later that I realized other non-Christian clubs were not the enemy. The devil was our enemy and the other clubs were to be the focus of our prayers and service.

Who has contended with you? Who is your enemy? Is it the police, the bank, a family member or business partner? Are you still ensnared by the painful memories of coming home from Viet Nam to an ungrateful country? Perhaps you are the survivor of an ugly divorce. When we are wronged, the sense of injustice can at times become overwhelming. It is difficult to know what to do with all of the resulting turmoil and we sometimes don't know which way to go. Sometimes we react….swiftly and decisively! We lash out, talk to anyone who will listen, kick the dog, yell at our families, curse, make threats, sabotage, manipulate, pick a fight or simply turn our anger inward and harm ourselves with drinking, gambling, eating, shopping or pornography.

All of these things are what can be referred to as unholy weapons of destruction. Yes, they are indeed able to destroy but they usually hit the wrong target or even blow up in our faces. The Apostle Paul tells the Christian in conflict: **"The weapons we fight with are not the weapons** of the world. On the contrary, they have divine power to demolish strongholds." (2Corinthians 10:4) Our weapons might include things like prayer, fasting, humility, communication and forgiveness. Easier said than done? Who received a more unjust sentence than Jesus Christ?

He was betrayed by his closest friends. His arrest and trial were illegal, a sham even by his accuser's standards. He was beaten to the point of being unrecognizable as a man. They shouted insults at him and spat on him and crucified him between two criminals. But what weapons did he use in his defense? **"He committed no sin, and no deceit was found in his mouth. When they hurled their insults at him he did not retaliate; when he suffered he made no threats. Instead, he entrusted himself to him who judges justly."** (1Peter 2:22-23)

The key to this Psalm is found in verse three. The writer implores God to **'say to my soul, "I am your salvation."'** He asks God to comfort his troubled soul and assure his spirit that he will be his help and vindicator. Just like Jesus, he trusts God to take care of his enemies but steadfastly refuses to formulate a retaliation plan of his own.

In fact, God's plan is that we would have a heart of grace and mercy towards those we feel have wronged us (See vs. 13-14). I have to be honest here and confess that I find it difficult to weep on behalf of someone who has injured me or someone I love. But if I truly desire God's heart, if I want to be great and not common, I can come to that place as I understand his character and unlimited capacity for love and forgiveness. That does not mean that I deny my feelings. It does not mean that the one who has wronged me has been let off of the hook. I simply make a choice to put it in a proper perspective-----not mine but God's. They and their rewards or punishments are in God's hands as he sees fit to deliver.

More times than not we have played at least a small part in the troubles that have come upon us. We are indeed imperfect sinners with mouths full of deceit or even violence. But when you are insulted, do not retaliate. When you suffer, make no threats. Instead, trust in God whose greater judgment is just.

Jesus said, 44 "... Love your enemies and pray for those who persecute you, 45 that you may be sons of your Father in heaven." Matthew 5:44-45

PSALM 36

Do You Always Dress Like That?

(Speaking of the wicked) *1 There is no fear of God before his eyes. 2 For in his own eyes he flatters himself too much to detect or hate his sin. 3 The words of his mouth are wicked and deceitful; he has ceased to be wise and to do good. 4 Even on his bed he plots evil; he commits himself to a sinful course and does not reject what is wrong. 5 Your love, O Lord, reaches to the heavens, your faithfulness to the skies. 6 Your righteousness is like the mighty mountains, your justice like the great deep. O Lord, you preserve both man and beast. 7 How priceless is your unfailing love! Both high and low among men find refuge in the shadow of your wings. 8 They feast on the abundance of your house; you give them drink from your river of delights. 9 For with you is the fountain of life; in your light we see light. 10 Continue your love to those who know you, your righteousness to the upright in heart. 11 May the foot of the proud not come against me, nor the hand of the wicked drive me away. 12 See how the evildoers lie fallen-thrown down, not able to rise!*

It was a cool Fall afternoon when my friend and I went for a short ride and ended up for lunch at a little place attractive to many in our area who just want to spend a leisurely few hours in a rural setting, listening to live music and sharing a bite to eat by the duck pond. Because of the winding country roads that lead to this semi-secret place, bikers and cyclists are especially attracted.

After lunch, my buddy got up to use the restroom. Within seconds I found myself listening to a conversation that came from the other side of the bushes behind me. I couldn't see the two men who were talking, but I was intrigued as they began to discuss my friend who had just walked past them. They were criticizing him for his leather coat, chaps, patched vest, long hair, tattoos and dark sunglasses. The exchange went something like this:

"Did you see that?" the one asked.

"See what?"

"That guy who just walked by," said the first. "Isn't that ridiculous? Can you imagine a grown man dressing like THAT in public? That is just ridiculous! You know they have all kinds of rituals associated with those vests and patches."

"Really?" encouraged the friend. "Like what?"

"Well, when they get that club patch, they sew it on a vest just like his. Then, before they can wear it officially they have to urinate on it in a special ceremony. They all do it!"

The second man gasped in disgust. (Personally, I was intrigued since no one had ever told me that I needed to pee on my vest!)

"Yeah", said the first, "Ya know those guys are all about drugs and orgies. All of the bikers are into that stuff!"

"Gee, that's really sad," said the friend.

I was partly angry and partly amused by the whole conversation and was pondering how funny it was that these guys didn't have a clue who my friend really was. He was a father, a grandfather, a faithful husband and a leader in his own church - and yet because of the way he was dressed and their own ignorance of the biker culture they had drawn some horribly inaccurate conclusions.

As the two men finished their lunch and got up to leave, I nearly choked on my burger as they walked by. Here they were, two overweight men, stuffed into spandex cycling pants and tight shirts. One was dressed in bright pink, the other in lime green. Each outfit also bore large bright letters, identifying the name of the suit's manufacturer. Their cycling shoes were made for the pedals of their bicycles so they were forced to walk on tippy toes to the parking lot. Little mushroom helmets were perched high upon their heads as they rode away. (Imagine! Grown men dressing like that in public!)

I suppose that it is human nature. We seldom see ourselves as others do and are quick to secretly judge them if only in our own minds. And while focused on self justification, we miss the obvious, that in our "**...own eyes** [we] **flatter** [ourselves] **too much to detect or hate** [our own] **sin.** " (v2) While our two bicycle friends were busy accusing all bikers of unsavory behavior, they missed the point that they themselves were guilty of gossip and false witness. How many times have we overlooked our own sin but were ready and willing to lash out against another?

The Psalmist encourages us: **"For with you** [God] **is the fountain of life; in your light we see light."** In other words, our job as Christians is to see others as God does; to see others through God's illuminated perspective and thus see more lovingly and clearly. Jesus cautioned us when he said, **"For in the same way you judge others,** you will be judged, and with the measure you use, it will be measured to you. Why do you look at the speck of sawdust in your brother's eye and pay no attention to the plank in your own eye? How can you say to your brother, 'Let me take the speck out of your eye,' when all the time there is a plank in your own eye?" (Matthew 7:2-4)

Perhaps our greater task is to **"fear God"** and seek to please him while at the same time, praying for others to be able to do the same. His love reaches to the heavens and his faithfulness to the skies. We, however, are sinners and desperately in need of a savior. We must have his love and faithfulness to lead fulfilled lives. And we need not be in everyone else's business, fine tuning their lives and filtering out all their imperfections. In whatever time we have left, we need to focus our attention on becoming more like Jesus ourselves.

———————————

But if we walk in the light, as he is in the light, we have fellowship with one another, and the blood of Jesus, his Son, purifies us from all sin." 1John 1:7

PSALM 37 8/30/13

OLD BIKERS NEVER DIE...

1 Do not fret because of evil men or be envious of those who do wrong; 2 for like the grass they will soon wither, like green plants they will soon die away. 3 Trust in the Lord and do good; dwell in the land and enjoy safe pasture. 4Delight yourself in the Lord and he will give you the desires of your heart. 5Commit your way to the Lord; trust in him and he will do this: 6 He will make your righteousness shine like the dawn, the justice of your cause like the noonday sun. 7 Be still before the Lord and wait patiently for him; do not fret when men succeed in their ways, when they carry out their wicked schemes. 8 Refrain from anger and turn from wrath; do not fret---it leads only to evil. 9 For evil men will be cut off, but those who hope in the Lord will inherit the land.

Life and the world in which we live is full of perilous stuff, and if that is not enough, we who read this book have probably chosen to ride motorcycles as well! We have added yet another dimension of danger to an already dangerous world.

I remember my friend John. We only rode together for a few years and when he died of kidney failure his riding buddies felt the loss. The next to go was Tom. We were riding through the mountains one Sunday afternoon when at one turn Tom just kept going straight...over the edge. We found out later that it wasn't the fall but a bad ticker that ended Tom's life. Others were hit by cars or passed away via natural causes. The point is, so many of them are gone and all of them are missed.

Remember when you were a kid? Do you remember…when you first got married…when you got your first bike…when you had kids of your own? Where has the time gone? Wasn't it just yesterday that we experienced Sturgis, South Dakota for the first time? We all "…**like the grass will soon wither, like green plants** [we] **will soon die"** like all of those who have gone before us.

I never had much time for history in school but lately I have enjoyed watching the history programs on television. The Civil War and World War II are my two favorite subjects. Once I even watched a series on the history of the motorcycle. But the most striking truth from observing history is that everyone before us is now gone. All of them! All of the people have withered like the grass. So, what makes us think that we will be any different? We too will soon be a part of Earth's history.

As we grow older we seek purpose in life (if we haven't already done so) and we seek peace for restless hearts that are full of unanswered questions. We ask, "Did my life count?" and "What will it be like to grow old…and die?" We ask ourselves, "What's on the other side?"

We are fortunate to have God's Word to read. In it we find truth for the mind, peace for the heart and direction for our lives. In this Psalm the writer gives us a six-point outline for better living and hope for tomorrow. Notice how we are not encouraged to work more, promote ourselves, look out for number one, get as much as we can or claw our way to the corporate top.   We are, however, instructed:

1.   Do not fret.
2.   Trust in the Lord.
3.   Delight yourself in the Lord.
4.   Commit your way to the Lord.
5.   Be still before the Lord.
6.   Refrain from anger.

As others wither, we are encouraged to not be afraid, but to trust in the Lord, even delight ourselves in his presence. A biker has the privilege of having his senses come alive while riding through creation. We see what great things God has made. We smell and feel the wind as it blows past our faces. We know the warmth of the sun and even the exhilaration of the cold as we roll down the highway. I say, delight yourself in the Lord and do not worry! If we are indeed his children, we will be with him forever.

There are so many that we meet on the road who claim to "know the man upstairs." Most "believe in God" but this Psalm tells us to **"commit** [our] **way to the Lord."** That means more than to have a mere knowledge of his existence. It means that his words are our code for the road. What he says is law and we know that it is good because nobody loves and cares for us as much as God.

Finally, just be still. Wait, listen, slow down and compare what we hear in our hearts with his written word. God will speak to us if we take the time to listen and he will lead us through every mile. And when life throws a curve ball, refrain from anger and begin again at the top…**"Do not fret…Trust in the Lord…Delight…"** yourself in him.

John and Tom and so many others are gone, but they knew God. They knew Jesus Christ as Lord and Savior! While it is true that they are absent from us, they are present with the Lord. They trusted in God for their salvation. They delighted in him daily and did not fret about their life after death. They committed not only their lives, but also their deaths to the Lord and we remember them and celebrate their memory.

There is a common saying among those who ride: "It's not the destination, but the journey that counts." While this may be true for a fast weekend on two wheels, it sadly misrepresents our life's journey. At the end of our road there is Heaven or Hell and only those who have committed their ways to the Lord will discover everlasting life. Furthermore, there are no guarantees as to when we will leave this world; could be tonight or perhaps tomorrow. We must, therefore, prepare NOW for that day, for we do not know when our time will come. All we can know for sure is that, according to history, IT IS coming. Are you ready?

Old bikers never die. They just begin a new journey.

———————————————————

27 Just as man is destined to die once, and after that to face judgment, 28 so Christ was sacrificed once to take away the sins of many people; and he will appear a second time, not to bear sin, but to bring salvation to those who are waiting for him.   Hebrews 9:27-28

PSALM 38

The Party's Over

---

1 O Lord, do not rebuke me in your anger or discipline me in your wrath. 2 For your arrows have pierced me, and your hand has come down upon me. 3 Because of your wrath there is no health in my body; my bones have no soundness because of my sin. 4 My guilt has overwhelmed me like a burden too heavy to bear. 5 My wounds fester and are loathsome because of my sinful folly. 6 I am bowed down and brought very low; all day long I go about mourning. 7 My back is filled with searing pain; there is no health in my body. 8 I am feeble and utterly crushed; I groan in anguish of heart. 9 All my longings lie open before you, O Lord; my sighing is not hidden from you. 10 My heart pounds, my strength fails me; even the light has gone from my eyes. 11 My friends and companions avoid me because of my wounds; my neighbors stay far away.

When he was younger, he could ride all day and party all night. His diet consisted of barbecue, cold beer and cigars. He never passed up a dare and took any bet whatever the odds. Sleep was optional, sunscreen a bother and his preferred ride was a hard tail no matter what it meant to his back the next morning. He had been married more than once and entertained more women than he could remember. He was 100% biker through and through.

Today his skin has been darkened by the sun and leathered by the wind. He is 50 pounds overweight, walks with a limp and suffers from a chronic cough. The years were hard and they went by fast. Today he is alone and left with more memories than friends. His name escapes me at the moment, but no matter, we all know ten men just like him. "If I had known I was going to live this long I would have taken better care of myself!" he jokes with the crowd.

As we read Psalm 38, we can't be exactly sure what David is talking about, but the bottom line is that his life has been hard and now he is paying the price. Furthermore, he has a deep sense of guilt for the previous years and fears that God's judgment will be severe. He describes himself as **"pierced"** and having **"no health"** in his body. His wounds **"fester"** because of his sinful folly and he is haunted by the fact that he has only himself to blame. Even his back **"is filled with searing pain"** and his friends are nowhere to be found.

Greater than any physical pain, however, the writer seems to be concerned with irreparable damage to his relationship with God in his twilight years. Getting older has a way of causing all of us human types to become introspective. **"All my longings lie open before you, O Lord."**

The good news is that God has no desire to rebuke us harshly. The greatest damage has been done by us to ourselves. God will never say, "I told you so." Instead, we can see the heart of the Father towards the prodigal in the Gospel of Luke, chapter fifteen. Like the old biker, this man's son had spent it all and was ready to come home. What is surprising is that we read, **"But while he was still a long way off, his father saw him and was filled with compassion for him."** (Luke 15:20)

God isn't mad at you or me - or the old biker! He's not even upset. On the contrary, he loves us! He is willing to take the ashes of our lives and turn them into something beautiful. We may still have a limp, but there is a light in our heart that will never go out because of his love and mercy. Come home. The Father is waiting and watching.

---

22 But the father said to his servants, "Quick! Bring the best robe and put it on him. Put a ring on his finger and sandals on his feet. 23 Bring the fattened calf and kill it. Let's have a feast and celebrate. 24 For this son of mine was dead and is alive again; he was lost and is found." So they began to celebrate.   Luke 15:22-24

P$\mathfrak{S}$AL$\mathfrak{M}$ 39

DUST IN THE WIND

4 Show me, O Lord, my life's end and the number of my days; let me know how fleeting is my life. 5 You have made my days a mere handbreadth; the span of my years is as nothing before you. Each man's life is but a breath. Selah 6 Man is a mere phantom as he goes to and fro: He bustles about, but only in vain; he heaps up wealth, not knowing who will get it. 7 But now, Lord, what do I look for? My hope is in you.

Most of us reading this book know exactly who Mr. Harley and Mr. Davidson were. They built a motorcycle that still dominates the market a hundred years after its inception. Likewise, Henry Ford was a man with an idea and his name still adorns millions of cars on the road today.

As humans we seem to have a desire for notoriety. We want to be somebody; a rock star, a racecar driver or a great businessperson. We desperately want to be remembered for something; being the fastest, the strongest, the richest or just the best known in our field. Rarely will history devote much time to the businessman who ALMOST made it or the private who marched at the end of the line. There are, however, millions of pages dedicated to the great scientists, inventors, CEO's and generals of history. And at the end of so many average people's lives they find themselves wanting to cry out like Brando, "I could have been somebody...I could have been a contender!"

Truthfully, relatively few of us will be remembered for very long after we are no longer living. Out of sight, out of mind has never been more true. Think about it ...can you name all four of your grandparents? ...first and last names? Maybe. How about naming all eight of your great grandparents? A little harder right? How many of us can name even two of our great great grandparents? Yet, you can bet they were no different from all of us and had the same yearning to make a lasting mark on their world. Yet, as hard as they may have tried, they are almost forgotten at the end of two generations unless they were unusually talented or notoriously bad.

In Psalm 39, the writer is asking God to give him an eternal perspective. He doesn't want to waste time on trivia ...on building something just to get his name on the front page of a newspaper. He notes correctly that man is a mere phantom. The picture here is steam from a kettle that is whistling and boiling away. It's making lots of noise and spraying a cloud of steam into the air that is visible to everyone in the room ...for a little less than two seconds before it evaporates forever into the atmosphere. (Just like your great grandparents.) My wife and I just returned from a two thousand mile motorcycle ride that took us through Yellowstone National Park. After waiting twenty minutes to see Old Faithful do its thing, all I could think of when it was over was, "Is that it?" How many of our lives conclude with a little steam and a little noise and a few cheers?

So then if it is so futile to seek a name for ourselves and collect titles, wealth and land, what should be the focus? We need to be rescued from this kind of present day thinking. Verse seven says it well....."**My hope is in you**" (the Lord). We need to be following the Lord Jesus and keeping our focus on Him...not on ourselves. When we do this, we get an eternal perspective and eternal life ...not a fleeting life that disappears as quickly as a cloud of steam. Our enemies will not be able to scoff and gloat over our finiteness if knowing God is our objective and end goal.

That's why verse twelve mentions that we dwell here as aliens because we don't buy into the same value system as the world in which we find ourselves. It means going against the grain in many cases. When we give up the search for importance and notoriety and think of ourselves as eternal beings with a much bigger purpose, and a much longer future (we will live forever...someplace), we can rejoice for we are free.

33b Provide purses for yourselves that will not wear out, a treasure in heaven that will not be exhausted, where no thief comes near and no moth destroys. 34 For where your treasure is, there your heart will be also.   Luke 12:33-34

PSALM 40

EVERY BIKER HAS AN OPINION...OR TWO

1 I waited patiently for the Lord; he turned to me and heard my cry. 2 He lifted me out of the slimy pit, out of the mud and mire; he set my feet on a rock and gave me a firm place to stand. 3 He put a new song in my mouth, a hymn of praise to our God. Many will see and fear and put their trust in the Lord. 4 Blessed is the man who makes the Lord his trust, who does not look to the proud, to those who turn aside to false gods. 5 Many, O Lord my God, are the wonders you have done. The things you planned for us no one can recount to you; were I to speak and tell of them, they would be too many to declare...9 I proclaim righteousness in the great assembly; I do not seal my lips...10 I do not hide your righteousness in my heart; I speak of your faithfulness and salvation. I do not conceal your love and your truth...

I've never known a biker to not have an opinion. Since we often find ourselves hanging out at a motorcycle shop or a restaurant, there's always an opportunity to talk politics, religion or just bike stuff. We'll argue helmet laws, windshields and which route to take to a favored destination. Add a few beers to the equation and the opinions become louder and bear more conviction.

I was leading twenty-five riders from Southern California to Oregon in the early Fall. As we met to stage at the gas station on the corner I had everyone gather up for a pre-ride meeting. I had been speaking for less than sixty seconds, describing our route from Southern California when a hand went up in the back. The suggestion was that the 15 freeway would be too crowded at this time of day and that we should take the 215. Before I could agree or disagree another offered up a rural route that would have taken longer but was more scenic. Soon the argument was time versus scenery while another debated safety. I never did finish that pre-ride meeting and made as few suggestions as possible for the next twenty-five hundred miles.

The opinionated biker does more than just argue his point. He prints his thoughts on tee-shirts and helmet stickers. If it's really important, he'll tattoo his convictions right on his flesh. Sometimes the results are bold and courageous and sometimes they are just disgusting and fowl, dishonoring of women and betraying the bearer's ignorance. So why is it that some can be so vocal about relative trivia and so silent when it comes to the important stuff - LIFE CHANGING stuff? Why is it so hard to talk about what God has done in our lives? We'll defend the American motorcycle against the metric but won't defend the name of Christ. We'll praise America in all of her glory and fight for her to the death but can't muster the courage to praise the name of our Lord and Savior. We are so tough and yet so fragile; so bold and yet cowards.

Whatever the reason, the biker community is full of people who have been **"lifted out of the slimy pit, out of the mud and mire."** Be it prison, drugs, alcohol, an ugly divorce or even recurring nightmares about fighting in a foreign land, God has lifted us up and **"set** [our] **feet on a rock**

and [given us] **a firm place to stand."** Why then are we so silent? Why won't we speak with as much passion for God and His goodness as we do about a motorcycle or a country?

Some will excuse themselves from such "fanaticism" and say that their religion is a private matter. But the psalmist tells us that our words of praise will help others **"see and fear and put their trust in the Lord."** And so in the end he concludes with a defiant proclamation, **"I do not seal my lips...I do not hide your righteousness...I do not conceal your love and your truth."**

C'mon tough guy! You dare to ride on two wheels at high speeds while others seek the security of an SUV. You've chosen to live your own life on your own terms and couldn't care less what some other drummer is beating. You are your own person when it comes to everything but that which is the most precious and important. God was there for you when you needed him the most and now are you afraid to speak up for him and for the others who need to hear about him?

I'm not suggesting that you quit your day job to become an evangelist. I don't think it's necessary for you to start riding with a LARGE BLACK BIBLE strapped to your ape-hangers. I'm just saying, "Speak up!" When the right time comes, say SOMETHING! Say what you think! Speak your mind! Be the voice of truth and reason when others say there is no hope. Live a life worthy of what God has done for you.

But in your hearts set apart Christ as Lord. Always be prepared to give an answer to everyone who asks you to give the reason for the hope that you have. 1Peter 3:15

PSALM 41

BROTHER FROM ANOTHER MOTHER

1 Blessed is he who has regard for the weak; the Lord delivers him in times of trouble. 2 The Lord will protect him and preserve his life; he will bless him in the land and not surrender him to the desire of his foes. 3 The Lord will sustain him on his sickbed and restore him from his bed of illness. 4 I said, "O Lord, have mercy on me; heal me, for I have sinned against you." 5 My enemies say of me in malice, "When will he die and his name perish?" 6 Whenever one comes to see me, he speaks falsely, while his heart gathers slander; then he goes out and spreads it abroad. 7 All my enemies whisper together against me; they imagine the worst for me, saying, 8 "A vile disease has beset him; he will never get up from the place where he lies." 9 Even my close friend, whom I trusted, he who shared my bread, has lifted up his heel against me. 10 But you, O Lord, have mercy on me; raise me up, that I may repay them. 11 I know that you are pleased with me, for my enemy does not triumph over me. 12 In my integrity you uphold me and set me in your presence forever. 13 Praise be to the Lord, the God of Israel, from everlasting to everlasting. Amen and Amen.

"I thought Bill was my friend," said Sean. "We had ridden many miles together, traded war stories and jokes and spent countless hours at the local Mexican restaurant laughing about our adventures on the road. We had attended too many rallies to count raising money for various charities. We even did a cross-country run with a dozen others just because we wanted to and had the time. I considered him a very good friend, someone that I could truly count on any time for anything. He was what we call, 'a brother from another mother.'"

Sean continued, "So it wasn't surprising that when I was in trouble, Bill came to see me. The bottom had fallen out for me in several different ways. I had lost my job, my family and was beginning to doubt my faith. I found myself pouring the whole story out to my friend along with all the sordid details, with the assumption that I was confiding in a trustworthy and caring advocate. I felt better after having done so and appreciated his prayers for me before he left.

A few days later, I began hearing rumors and some of my other friends began to share things with me that really shook me up. Some of what I was hearing were things I had told only one person - Bill! I couldn't believe it! This 'brother' with whom I had spent so much time and shared so many miles and experiences, wasn't a true and trustworthy friend after all! He took my pain and turned it into juicy little tidbits of gossip for casual chatter. He betrayed me for the opportunity to tell a good story. I'm not sure if I will ever be able to trust people with my thoughts and feelings again."

Sean's story is not unique. We've all been disappointed by a close friend. They broke confidentiality and betrayed us with their words to others. That's what verse six talks about, **"Whenever one comes to see me, he speaks falsely, while his heart gathers slander; then he goes out and spreads it abroad."** We expect to be slashed by our enemies or competitors, but the wounds of a friend cut deeper and are more painful than any other and if they profess to be a Christian, the injustice seems even worse.

I have counseled with many who have suffered such a betrayal. They often go on to indict a whole group of people by saying, "Those bikers…" or "Those Christians…" but the fact is that people are people! There are good ones and bad ones and we need to learn how to recognize who is safe and who is not. God is most assuredly a safe place for us and he blesses those who are trustworthy with the feelings and vulnerabilities of those who are down and out: **"Blessed is he who has regard for the weak; the Lord delivers him in times of trouble."**

This Psalm assures us that God is indeed our protector and true friend. He **"protects…preserves…blesses…**[and] **sustains"** his people. Our only contribution is to remain real with God, confessing our sins and striving to be men and women of integrity. The promise that we have from Christ is that he will never leave us or abandon us in our time of trouble. That doesn't mean that he will condone our behavior, but that he will love us no matter what; convicting our hearts of sin and encouraging us towards righteous living. Jesus never stopped loving his disciples even though they all deserted him in his time of need. People are people; weak, selfish and self-centered (just like you and me), but God is a friend who sticks closer than a brother - even a brother from another mother.

---

17 And I pray that you, being rooted and established in love, 18 may have power, together with all the saints, to grasp how wide and long and high and deep is the love of Christ. Ephesians 3:17-18

150

PSALM 42

WHERE IS YOUR GOD?

1 As the deer pants for streams of water, so my soul pants for you, O God. 2 My soul thirsts for God, for the living God. When can I go and meet with God? 3 My tears have been my food day and night, while men say to me all day long, "Where is your God?" 4 These things I remember as I pour out my soul: how I used to go with the multitude, leading the procession to the house of God, with shouts of joy and thanksgiving among the festive throng. 5 Why are you downcast, O my soul? Why so disturbed within me? Put your hope in God, for I will yet praise him, my Savior and my God.

8 By day the Lord directs his love, at night his song is with me - a prayer to the God of my life. 9 I say to God my Rock, "Why have you forgotten me? Why must I go about mourning, oppressed by the enemy?" 10 My bones suffer mortal agony as my foes taunt me, saying to me all day long, "Where is your God?" 11 Why are you downcast, O my soul? Why so disturbed within me? Put your hope in God, for I will yet praise him, my Savior and my God.

I have always thought of bikers as being "spiritual" people, but have met very few who are "religious." By "spiritual" I mean that they seem to be in search of that someone or something that is higher than and more worthy than themselves. For me, that would be the god of the Old and New Testaments; Jesus Christ, King of kings and Lord of lords. For those who have yet to discover Christ, they often speak of "the man upstairs." Some will carry charms or crystals in an effort to "plug in" to the celestial power and few will miss the opportunity to have their bike "blessed" by a pastor or priest. However they choose to express it, bikers for the most part are spiritual.

A group of us Christian fanatical types were in Laughlin, Nevada for the big "River Run" weekend. We wanted to do something to express our faith, but strategically were stumped on how to go about connecting with 80,000 riders. We settled on what we later called a, "Mobile Blessing of the Bikes." In groups of three we would work our way through the parking lots, looking for those who were just coming in or about to leave on their scoots. As we approached them and greeted them we said, "We're doing a mobile blessing of the bikes. It doesn't cost anything and takes about three minutes. Are you interested?" Our experience revealed that 70% of all the people we approached appreciated the opportunity to have some "magic" sprinkled over their machine.

As we proceeded with our bike blessing, some stood silent and respectful while others smoked a cigarette and stared off into the desert. A few actually began to weep as we prayed that God would bless them and their motorcycle, protecting them from breakdown and injury. They seemed especially moved when we would (in some cases) lay our hands on them and pray that they would come to a place of awareness of a loving god and inner peace. Of the 30% who declined our offer, most were in a big hurry to meet someone or get someplace. Only one or two blatantly rejected the "spiritual" opportunity and just one had an angry curse of disapproval.

I tell this story because I believe that many of those bikers whom we prayed for that day were a lot like David, the writer of this psalm. They would never think to put it this way, but their souls panted for God. They thirsted like an animal that has been running for his life. Something inside of them haunted them, asking, "Where is your God?" and only a very few could settle for being mere atheists. People who do not have a relationship with someone greater than themselves, find that there is something missing in their lives; a giant god shaped hole waiting to be filled.

David, like too many of us, was under a siege of problems. Circumstances and people were coming at him so fast that he who was once described as "a man after God's own heart" became confused and actually believed that God had forgotten him. He had once bragged on God in his songs but now his enemies were taunting him, "Where is your God now David?" The only hint of hope and sanity in this chapter is when David asks, **"Why are you downcast, O my soul? Why so disturbed within me? Put your hope in God, for I will yet praise him, my savior and my God."**

The truth is, God never did abandon David and he has never abandoned us. In fact, he was there when we were born and has never moved. He was there when we took our first steps and with us during our first day of school. He was there when we looked at that first bike and said, "Wow! I want one!" And he was there more times than we realize, protecting us from distracted drivers and road debris. It is we who have wandered away in pursuit of doing our own thing. But he's still there! He always has been!

You have stopped to look at a beautiful sunset and wondered… You have felt the desert breeze in your face in the early morning and thought… could it be God? Yes! That's him. He's there. He is not in the bell dangling from your frame or in the charm hanging around your neck. He's not "the man upstairs." He's standing right next to you and he is God Almighty, revealed through his Son Jesus Christ. He is your God. Bow down and worship him.

And without faith it is impossible to please God, because anyone who comes to him must believe that he exists and that he rewards those who earnestly seek him.   Hebrews 11:6

PSALM 43

STORMS OF INJUSTICE

---

1 Vindicate me, O God, and plead my cause against an ungodly nation; rescue me from deceitful and wicked men. 2 You are God my stronghold. Why have you rejected me? Why must I go about mourning, oppressed by the enemy? 3 Send forth your light and your truth, let them guide me; let them bring me to your holy mountain, to the place where you dwell. 4 Then will I go to the altar of God, to God, my joy and my delight. I will praise you with the harp, O God, my God. 5 Why are you downcast, O my soul? Why so disturbed within me? Put your hope in God, for I will yet praise him, my Savior and my God.

He was one of the nicest guys you'd ever want to meet, but suddenly and without warning, his warm eyes and friendly smile could turn into rage and cursing. It destroyed his first and second marriage and was putting a tremendous strain upon the third. What should have been lifelong friendships lasted weeks, months at best. Each week he would return to the VA hospital to plead his cause to a therapist against an ungodly nation who had rejected his offering of service and the ultimate sacrifice of thousands. He was a Vietnam vet.

Many of those who ride today are brave men and women who returned as unwelcome heroes from the Vietnam War. They fought and served their country well only to be jeered at and spit upon by those whom they were sent to defend. Today, however, tens of thousands ride across the country to remember the sacrifices of those who died or failed to return home.

The world is full of injustice whether you speak of war or have simply been laid off from your job. Perhaps you are the victim of an unjust lawsuit or have been shocked to discover first hand that racism still abounds in the 21st century. An ungodly nation is most easily recognized by its injustices. Nations however, are made up of mere men, sometimes wicked men whose motives and intentions are fueled by greed and self-preservation. And here you stand, one man or one woman, caught in the storms of injustice.

Since the end of World War II, combat weary soldiers have returned looking for a sense of escape and camaraderie on a motorcycle. Speed can change a lot of things and life looks better when the sun is on your back and the wind is in your face. Country roads winding out in front of you can lead riders to a place of serenity and calm. Many use this opportunity to thumb their noses at the world and leave their cares behind. Even today's businessman can gain new perspective on a hectic day with a one hour lunch break that includes a brief ride and a sense of freedom from corporate tyranny. But when the ride is over, the world and all of its injustice remains firmly intact.

The writer of Psalm 43 has a specific destination in mind for his ride; **"Your holy mountain, to the place where you dwell...to the alter of God."** It is there that he is promised that he will find more than a brief interlude, but rather two cosmic principles that bring a lasting sense of justice and peace.

First, there is **light** from which we gain a greater understanding for how things truly are and not just how they seem. Have you ever stared at an object in the dark, sure that it was an intruder, only to be revealed in the light as a pair of slacks tossed across the back of a chair? Light has a way of revealing the truth. As we struggle each day in the world's trenches and valleys, we can gain a greater peace by looking through the eyes of God. When we gain his perspective our enemies are not nearly as fearsome and large. Chaos and confusion are lessened by the light. Jesus said, **"I am the light of the world."**

The second prize that comes from being in God's presence is **truth.** Not truth spun by a network to accommodate the latest news headline or a politician's platform, but pure truth with no ulterior motive but love. Such godly perspective brings about not only clarity for the moment but strength for perseverance. When you know the truth, **"the truth shall set you free."** Shall we then be free from all injustice and unfairness? Never, this side of Heaven - but we will be free from hopelessness and a sense of being alone.

When it all becomes too much, when you have a cause to plead and when you need rescuing from deceitful and wicked men, bring your case to God through prayer. He is your God...your **joy**...your **delight**. In him you will find a refuge and a stronghold of perspective and truth. Let these guide you. And ask yourself, **"Why are you downcast... why so disturbed?** Put your hope in God.

"In this world you will have trouble. But take heart! I have overcome the world."   John 16:33

PSALM 44

RIDING HIGH

1 We have heard with our ears, O God; our fathers have told us what you did in their days, in days long ago. 2 With your hand you drove out the nations and planted our fathers; you crushed the peoples and made our fathers flourish. 3 It was not by their sword that they won the land, nor did their arm bring them victory; it was your right hand, your arm, and the light of your face, for you loved them. 4 You are my King and my God, who decrees victories for Jacob. 5 Through you we push back our enemies; through your name we trample our foes. 6 I do not trust in my bow, my sword does not bring me victory; 7 but you give us victory over our enemies, you put our adversaries to shame. 8 In God we make our boast all day long, and we will praise your name forever.

He was a pretty cool guy! He wore denim and leather (what else?) and practically lived behind his dark glasses. He rode a wild horse made of chrome and steel, saddled with exotic paint and a custom sharkskin seat. With hands raised high on eighteen-inch apes and legs extended to reach the highway pegs, he looked real impressive rolling down the road, always heralded by the rumble and growl of his twin fishtails. Yep! He was one bad hombre. He was smart and successful and at the top of his field. Furthermore, he had done it all his own way! He's what we call "a self made man." So, how come he needed to borrow twenty bucks for lunch? Because he was broke! His self-made world had come crashing down around him. It could have been any of us.

Do you think that your above average intelligence has gotten you where you are today? Are you proud that your business savvy has made you lots of money? Are you secretly of the opinion that your physical strength and intimidating manner has somehow scared off a formidable enemy? Forget about it! Those attitudes are called pride and have little to do with the triumphs we experience in life. We simply haven't got that much going for us. It is God who deserves the lion's share of the credit for blessing us and pulling us through good and bad times. Bill Gates, Donald Trump and yes, even Willie G. Davidson have been blessed and favored by God.

In the Old Testament, it was God that defeated the enemies of the Hebrews. **"With your hand you drove out the nations and planted our fathers; you crushed the peoples and made our fathers flourish. "** It was not their strength of numbers or wisdom in battle. **"...it was your right hand, your arm, and the light of your face..."** David had the right perspective: **"You are my King and my God...Through you we push back our enemies; through your name we trample our foes."** He did not trust his resources and knew that it was not anything of himself that brought him success.

Take a breath...and give God thanks for it. If you have a home and people who love you...give God thanks. If you have a job or money in the bank, know that God is the provider. If you have composed a song or written a book, or even had a bright idea...give God the glory. If you have the time, strength and ability to ride a motorcycle, give God thanks. For everything that you see on your ride; the sky, the trees, the mountains and the river, give him the praise. "**In God we make our boast all day long, and we will praise your name forever.** "

---

16 Don't be deceived, my dear brothers. 17 Every good and perfect gift is from above, coming down from the Father of the heavenly lights, who does not change like shifting shadows. James 1:16-17

PSALM 45

RIDING WITH A GREATER PURPOSE

1 My heart is stirred by a noble theme as I recite my verses for the king; my tongue is the pen of a skillful writer. 2 You are the most excellent of men and your lips have been anointed with grace, since God has blessed you forever. 3 Gird your sword upon your side, O mighty one; clothe yourself with splendor and majesty. 4 In your majesty ride forth victoriously in behalf of truth, humility and righteousness; let your right hand display awesome deeds. 5 Let your sharp arrows pierce the hearts of the king's enemies; let the nations fall beneath your feet. 6 Your throne, O God, will last forever and ever; a scepter of justice will be the scepter of your kingdom. 7 You love righteousness and hate wickedness; therefore God, your God, has set you above your companions by anointing you with the oil of joy.

There are a lot of reasons that I love to ride. The wind, the sun and the surge and sound of power that explodes from a big v-twin are just a few. My favorite thing about being a rider however, is the sense of purpose and mission that we seem to have as a community of two wheelers. It is no secret that bikers across the country have raised hundreds of millions of dollars for the homeless, education, medical research and children. Furthermore, if one of our own goes down and is injured, it isn't long before several thousand dollars have been collected for them and their family. As an organizer of motorcycle events, I can attest to the fact

that bikers are some of the most generous people in the world. We all enjoy a weekend ride or a cross-country adventure, but nothing is as rewarding as riding with a purpose.

As Christian bikers, we enjoy all of the above and more! Not only do we ride for the underprivileged and sick, we ride for the lost and hopeless as well. We too appreciate raising money for a cause or a cure or an opportunity to deliver a Christmas toy to a child, but "**My heart is stirred by a noble theme**" as I throw a leg across the saddle! With Christ, those of us who are called according to his purpose, "**ride forth victoriously in behalf of truth, humility and righteousness**" and we pray that his "**right hand display awesome deeds.**" It's good to ride for a good cause, but it is the ultimate thrill to ride and know that you do so in the name of God and for his ultimate glory! Nobody ever loved and cared for the poor and sick like Jesus did, but Jesus doesn't stop there! His heart burns for much more.

When we give a child a toy, its healing power is limited by time and rust. If a hungry person is fed today, they will be hungry tomorrow. Even if a sick person is cured, they will, in the end, return to the dust from which they came. While all of these acts of kindness should continue, there is more that we can give! Christians ride with the Good News that there is indeed a God who loves this world and has given his Son Jesus Christ as the ultimate sacrifice for us! Our Good News is that they need not ever be spiritually hungry or thirsty again, for Jesus has said, "**I am the bread of life**" and "**He who comes to me will never thirst!**" Even to the terminally ill we can bring the hope of eternal life for Jesus has commissioned us to do so.

The psalmist says of Christ, **"You are the most excellent of men and your lips have been anointed with grace, since God has blessed you forever. Gird your sword upon your side, O mighty one; clothe yourself with splendor and majesty."** How amazing is it that we would be invited to ride alongside Jesus Christ? We bring gifts in Jesus' name! We bless your bikes in Jesus' name and bring prayers for health and well being. We ride as ambassadors of truth and justice in Jesus' name. And we do not ride alone - ever! Jesus, this **"most excellent of men"** - who is the Son of God - goes with us. No mere fundraiser or toy run has ever been so great, so meaningful, so effective or so timeless. Ride with a greater purpose my friends! Ride with God!

---

18 All authority in heaven and on earth has been given to me. 19 Therefore go and make disciples of all nations, baptizing them in the name of the Father and of the Son and the Holy Spirit, 20 and teaching them to obey everything I have commanded you. And surely I am with you always, to the very end of the age.   Matthew 28:18-20

Psalm 46

A Leg Up On Reality

---

1 God is our refuge and strength, an ever-present help in trouble. 2 Therefore we will not fear, though the earth give way and the mountains fall into the heart of the sea, 3 though its waters roar and foam and the mountains quake with their surging. Selah

7 The Lord Almighty is with us; the God of Jacob is our fortress. Selah 8 Come and see the works of the Lord, the desolations he has brought on the earth. 9 He makes wars cease to the ends of the earth; he breaks the bow and shatters the spear, he burns the shields with fire. 10 "Be still, and know that I am God; I will be exalted among the nations, I will be exalted in the earth." 11 The Lord Almighty is with us; the God of Jacob is our fortress.

Have you ever been in a place where your reality was challenged and suddenly the world as you knew it seemed to radically shift? Earthquakes can have that effect. What we once knew to be terra firma is now violently shifting and shaking and seriously threatening our perception and sense of security.

A group of our friends were taking a leisurely Sunday ride up into the foothills to enjoy some cool air and sunshine. Marcy was at the rear of the pack, staggered behind Roy who was riding his new bike. As the group rounded a curve, Roy cut it a little sharp and grazed the side of a temporary white wall...the kind the highway department uses during its construction projects.

No one had informed Marcy that Roy had a prosthetic leg. The relatively mild impact against the wall was enough to send Roy off balance, dislodge the limb and send it flying right into Marcy's path where it landed with a dull thud. Sure that her downed comrade had lost a perfectly good leg, reality suddenly shifted, because these things just are not supposed to pop off! As she made a quick stop, panic got the best of her and she began to scream hysterically until the truth settled in and her understanding of what had actually happened was readjusted. It didn't help, however, as one of the sick humored friends picked up Roy's prosthesis and used it to direct traffic around the scene of the accident. We all laugh about it now, but for a few moments, Marcy's world was in chaos.

There are a lot of things that we perceive to be reality and therefore rely on as places of security. Health, wealth and common conveniences lure us into believing that all is well and good. The truth is, however, that at any moment the ground can begin to shake and our world can be turned upside down with a heart attack, a natural disaster or a shift in the stock market. If the ground that we stand on cannot be trusted then where can we go to find security and peace of mind?

As Christians, our **"refuge and strength"** come from God and he is our **"ever-present help in trouble."** Though, **"the earth give way and the mountains fall into the heart of the sea"** (or life begins to unravel), God comforts us with, " **Be still and know that I am God…**" And we can proclaim, "The Lord Almighty is with us…"

Times change and things happen and life is very good at throwing curve balls, but God is more dependable than the rising and setting of the sun. He has assured us time and again in scripture that he will never leave us or forsake us. Wherever you are right now, whatever you are doing and whatever the news man said this morning, God has not changed. He has not been moved or shaken. He has always been and always will be and he is waiting there for you today.

---

24 Therefore everyone who hears these words of mine and puts them into practice is like a wise man who built his house on the rock. 25 The rain came down, the streams rose, and the winds blew and beat against that house; yet it did not fall, because it had its foundation on the rock. Mathew 7:24-25

PSALM 47

LASTING BROTHERHOOD

---

1 Clap your hands, all you nations; shout to God with cries of joy. 2 How awesome is the Lord Most High, the great King over all the earth! 3 He subdued nations under us, peoples under our feet. 4 He chose our inheritance for us, the pride of Jacob, whom he loved. Selah 5 God has ascended amid shouts of joy, the Lord amid the sounding of trumpets. 6 Sing praises to God, sing praises; sing praises to our King, sing praises. 7 For God is the King of all the earth; sing to him a psalm of praise. 8 God reigns over the nations; God is seated on his holy throne. 9 The nobles of the nations assemble as the people of the God of Abraham, for the kings of the earth belong to God; he is greatly exalted.

There's an old joke familiar to church folks that comes from the assumption that in any children's Sunday School class the answer to almost any question is going to be "Jesus." The joke, therefore, goes something like this: "The Sunday School teacher was telling her ten year olds about God's creatures one morning when she asked, 'What's gray, lives in a tree, has a big fluffy tail and eats nuts?' To which one little boy said, 'Well, it sounds a lot like a squirrel, but I'll say Jesus!'"

My pastor had a similar experience while speaking before a group of clergymen. He told this story: "I went to a meeting the other night and the room was filled with people. In the crowd there were old people and young people, men and women. Represented were singles and couples, several races, successful business professionals and the current jobless. There were those who were rich and those who could barely make ends meet. Some were educated and some were not. They were a diverse bunch to say the least. But they talked and laughed and seemed to have a good time. They ate, drank coffee and told stories with great gusto, slapping each other on the back. The purpose for their gathering was clear to the outsider. They had come because of one great name; a name that is recognized and revered around the world!" And then my pastor asked the congregation, "You know what that name is, don't you?" To which the audience replied in chorus, "JESUS!" But the pastor corrected, "No! The name is Harley-Davidson." And a shock of silence and a sense of sacrilege blanketed the crowd because they did not realize that he was describing a HOG meeting.

It's funny how so many people with so many differences could come together and get along, even enjoy one another just because they all ride the same motorcycle. They share ideas and experiences and end up discovering unity. Any other time and place they might have been tempted to polarize because of their diversity, but here, on this night, the name of Harley-Davidson has brought them together.

Christians should be like that too! We come from all colors and all nations. We live in a penthouse in Manhattan and in a brush covered hut in the Sudan. We are men and women, rich and poor, young and old. But when we come together, we smile and we celebrate one great name. This time, however, the name is Jesus; a name that is far greater than any motorcycle, even if it is a legend.

So often we see Christianity as a religion for Americans in the twenty-first century. Truth be told, we have been around since the Apostle Peter first declared of Jesus, "You are the Christ!" God is calling people from all tribes, all colors and nations! He is **the great King over all the earth** and **"reigns over the nations."** Therefore, the writer of this psalms invites, **"Clap your hands, all you nations; shout to God with cries of joy."**

For some, there is a deep sense of pride and brotherhood that arises as their national anthem is sung and their flag is raised. For bikers, there is a camaraderie that wells up within us when we pass another on the road and offer the "low down" salute. But for the Christian, it is the name of our God and the awareness of his unique greatness that causes our hearts to race, our differences to fade and our praises to flow. His majesty cannot be compared with anything, not even a nation. He stands alone as the King of all kings and the Lord of all lords.

"You are worthy to take the scroll and to open its seals, because you were slain, and with your blood you purchased men for God from every tribe and language and people and nation." Revelation 5:9

PSALM 48

ROAD CAPTAIN

1 Great is the Lord, and most worthy of praise, in the city of our God, his holy mountain. 2 It is beautiful in its loftiness, the joy of the whole earth...

8 As we have heard, so have we seen in the city of the Lord Almighty, in the city of our God: God makes her secure forever. Selah 9 Within your temple, O God, we meditate on your unfailing love. 10 Like your name, O God, your praise reaches to the ends of the earth; your right hand is filled with righteousness...

14 For this God is our God for ever and ever; he will be our guide even to the end.

I have a friend that is known by many as "Back Roads." If there is an alternative, out-of-the-way route to be taken, he will find it. Back Roads will avoid city traffic and congested freeways every chance he gets in favor of some obscure but beautiful country road that will meander for miles without ever revealing a signpost or landmark that might lend a clue as to where we are. Just when we have all concluded that we are hopelessly lost, we emerge at an intersection just a short distance from our desired destination.

There is a romantic sentiment among bikers: "It's not the destination, it's the ride." We who ride know what

172

that means and so does Back Roads! It means that the journey and how we get there is as important as arriving. It means that the privilege of riding in the open air while we smell and embrace nature, maximizes the end of the day. Traveling in a car or a bus from place to place is something that some choose to endure in order to celebrate their destination. Our travel, however, is our celebration and the arrival is but a place to rest before returning to the saddle for another day

I always enjoy riding with Back Roads because all I have to do is sit back and enjoy the ride. While he carefully navigates us through a forest or a series of rolling hills, I'm simply enjoying the view and the roar of my motor. I trust him as a road captain because he has never let me down.

God has the same reputation with those of us who have followed him for years. He tells us again and again that he has a "road less traveled" for those who will trust him. It can be disconcerting at times, but when you have confidence in the one who is leading, you are free to enjoy the ride.

We often say of him, **"Great is the Lord, and most worthy of praise!"** We recognize our security when we are with him and under are his care. We openly and proudly declare, **"This God is our God for ever and ever; he will be our guide even to the end."**

When Jesus spoke again to the people, he said, "I am the light of the world. Whoever follows me will never walk in darkness, but will have the light of life." John 8:12

PSALM 49

THE LAST RIDE

*1 Hear this, all you peoples; listen, all who live in this world,
2 both low and high, rich and poor alike: 3 My mouth will
speak words of wisdom; the utterance from my heart will give
understanding. 4 I will turn my ear to a proverb; with the
harp I will expound my riddle: 5 Why should I fear when
evil days come, when wicked deceivers surround me - 6 those
who trust in their wealth and boast of their great riches? 7 No
man can redeem the life of another or give to God a ransom
for him - 8 the ransom for a life is costly, no payment is ever
enough- 9 that he should live on forever and not see decay. 10
For all can see that wise men die; the foolish and the senseless
alike perish and leave their wealth to others.*

*15 But God will redeem my life from the grave; he will surely
take me to himself. Selah 16 Do not be overawed when a man
grows rich, when the splendor of his house increases; 17 for
he will take nothing with him when he dies, his splendor will
not descend with him. 18 Though while he lived he counted
himself blessed - and men praise you when you prosper- 19 he
will join the generation of his fathers, who will never see the
light of life. 20 A man who has riches without understanding
is like the beasts that perish.*

I love to ride. I love just about everything having to do
with motorcycles. I also love having friends who appreciate
bikes as much as I do. Therein, however, lies the one thing
that I don't enjoy about riding. I have had more than one
friend end up on the bad side of an accident and been

injured, some even killed. Every time I happen upon the scene of a motorcycle accident, I'm afraid to look for fear that it will be someone I know.

Some go down because they made a mistake in their judgment. Others fall victim to someone else's stupidity or carelessness. Either way, they are just as injured or even dead. In fact, we all end up dead. I've been watching the history channel on TV lately. One thing these stories have in common, from the American Revolution to the Civil War, both rich and poor, great and small, all of the players are dead today. One bumper sticker reads, "None of us are getting out of this [life] alive."

Even if we do survive twenty or thirty years of riding the freeways, there is always cancer, heart attacks and if nothing else, old age. We will all join **"the generation of his fathers."** The question is, "Are we prepared for this last ride?"

For those who do not believe in God and the grace and mercy that come from knowing his son, Jesus Christ, there is no hope to **"see the light of life."** But for those who do put their trust in Christ, **"God will redeem my life from the grave; he will surely take me to himself."** For the **"beasts that perish"** there is nothing. Even for the wealthiest and most prosperous of humans there is nothing to be celebrated after death without Christ. **"A man who has riches without understanding is like the beasts that perish."** And what is it that we are to understand? That none of us will take anything with us when we die. All of the most beautiful motorcycles in the world and their saddlebags stuffed with gold will ever go any farther than the grave. Likewise, fame, fortune and success cease to benefit us when the heart stops beating. The most powerful and influential of men and women in history have nothing that will serve them in death. Their splendor **"will not descend"** with them.

As you prepare for this last ride, what will you put in your saddlebags? Silver and gold? Power and affluence? Better to have wisdom and understanding, confession and humility before your Maker. We've heard it many times before and laughed, "Chrome won't get you home." Never has it been more true than now. We need Jesus if we ever expect to make it to our eternal destination.

---

19 Do not store up for yourselves treasures on earth, where moth and rust destroy, and where thieves break in and steal. 20 But store up for yourselves treasures in heaven, where moth and rust do not destroy, and where thieves do not break in and steal. 21 For where your treasure is, there your heart will be also.   Matthew 6:19-21

PSALM 50

IF I HAVE TO EXPLAIN, YOU WOULDN'T UNDERSTAND

1 *The Mighty One, God, the LORD, speaks and summons the earth from the rising of the sun to the place where it sets. 2 From Zion, perfect in beauty, God shines forth. 3 Our God comes and will not be silent; a fire devours before him, and around him a tempest rages 4 He summons the heavens above, and the earth, that he may judge his people: 5 "Gather to me my consecrated ones, who made a covenant with me by sacrifice." 6 And the heavens proclaim his righteousness, for God himself is judge. Selah 7"Hear, O my people, and I will speak, O Israel, and I will testify against you: I am God, your God. 8 I do not rebuke you for your sacrifices or your burnt offerings, which are ever before me. 9 I have no need of a bull from your stall or of goats from your pens, 10 for every animal of the forest is mine, and the cattle on a thousand hills. 11 I know every bird in the mountains, and the creatures of the field are mine. 12 If I were hungry I would not tell you, for the world is mine, and all that is in it.*

16 *But to the wicked, God says: "What right have you to recite my laws or take my covenant on your lips? 17 You hate my instruction and cast my words behind you. 18 When you see a thief, you join with him; you throw in your lot with adulterers. 19 You use your mouth for evil and harness your tongue to deceit. 20 You speak continually against your brother and slander your own mother's son. 21 These things you have done and I kept silent; you thought I was altogether like you. But I will rebuke you and accuse you to your face.*

22 Consider this, you who forget God, or I will tear you to pieces, with none to rescue: 23 He who sacrifices thank offerings honors me, and he prepares the way so that I may show him the salvation of God."

Biker rallies are great places to find things you didn't know you wanted or needed. Everything bikeresque can be had for a price including clothing, leather, accessories, jewelry, body art and the ever-present catchy slogan which has been embroidered, silk-screened or etched. This is to insure that one's philosophy on life, the opposite sex, laws and politics can be readily identified wherever you go whether or not you choose to speak. One such phrase has appeared on everything from tee shirts to helmet stickers. It attempts to express the reason we love to ride but also seems fitting when we seek to put into words the wonders of our God: "If I have to explain, you wouldn't understand!"

Here we are at the end of our first fifty Psalms of the Old Testament. We've talked about God's greatness and mercy, his faithfulness and protection in times of need and even about his holiness. But we conclude this first volume with one absolute, non-negotiable truth that towers over us like a solid granite monolith which is unmoved by the winds of time and the progression of man. The first few verses read almost like a challenge: **The Mighty One…GOD…the LORD, speaks and summons…[He] comes and will not be silent; a fire devours before him, and around him a tempest rages, and the earth, that he may judge his people…I am God, your God!"** The Psalmist is doing his best to verbalize the greatness of God but seems to labor to find just the right words for one who is so awe inspiring. After all, how can a limited language and a finite mind adequately express the wonders of our God and the author of the universe? He seems to be thinking, "If I have to explain you wouldn't understand."

We want for you to know, here at the end of this book, that God is not negotiable. He is indeed a god of love and compassion, mercy and forgiveness, but he is nonetheless, GOD! He does not need us, but he wants us. We are not his equals, but he welcomes us into his presence. He loves us just the way we are, but too much to leave us that way. He will not tolerate sin in any form and demands that we come to him with a broken and contrite heart, on our knees in humble submission with a full confession. He is not "the man upstairs" or "the cosmic Santa Claus" who gives us everything we want. He is GOD the Father and we are at his invitation his adopted children.

He is not impressed with our religious rhetoric or business. We usually think of the wicked as the liars, murderers and criminals in society but the **"wicked"** spoken of in verse sixteen are church going folks. Who else would recite God's laws or speak of his covenants? He demands more than religion. He craves communion and companionship with us! He gave his son Jesus Christ to die on the cross that our sins might be forgiven and a right relationship with him may be restored.

May we challenge you to begin the journey today if you have not already done so? God invites you to experience the open road with him. Saddle up and prepare for the ride of your life. You may not be able to explain it, but finally you will understand.

13 *When Jesus came to the region of Caesarea Philippi, he asked his disciples, "Who do people say the Son of Man is?"* 14 *They replied, "Some say John the Baptist; others say Elijah; and still others, Jeremiah or one of the prophets."* 15 *"But what about you?" he asked. "Who do you say I am?"* 16 *Simon Peter answered, "You are the Christ, the Son of the living God."* Matthew 16:13-16

1838389R00104

Made in the USA
San Bernardino, CA
07 February 2013